What They *Really* Said series
Edited by A. N. GILKES

WHAT MARX *REALLY* SAID

H. B. ACTON

WHAT
MARX
REALLY
SAID

Schocken Books · New York

Published in the United States of America in 1967
by Schocken Books Inc., 67 Park Avenue, New York, N.Y. 10016

Contents

Preface

determine

As the object of this book is to ascertain what Marx really did say rather than what he might have said or is reputed to have said, I have gone to the original German text (or in the case of *The Poverty of Philosophy* the original French text) and made my own translations from that. In doing this I have tried to be as literal as possible rather than to aim at elegance of style.　　　　　H. B. Acton.

WHAT MARX *REALLY* SAID

I   The Origins of Marxism

§1   *Marx and Engels and the Publication of* The
     Communist Manifesto *of 1848*

Marxism, both as a theory and as a social and political
movement, was created by Karl Marx and Friedrich
Engels in collaboration with one another. They began
working together in 1844 and their first joint production
was a book called *The Holy Family* which was published
in Stuttgart in 1845. Marx had written most of this, but
Engels contributed a great deal to *The German Ideology*
which was written in 1845–6 but not published until long
after they were both dead. The famous *Communist
Manifesto* (1848) was put together by Marx from a draft,
much of which he ignored, given to him by Engels and
was published as their joint work.[1] If we start by tracing
the separate careers of these two men and by seeing how
they came to join forces, we shall obtain a preliminary
view of what Marxism is and what it sets out to do.

Karl Marx was born at Trier in the Rhineland, then a
part of Prussia, in 1818. He was the son of Jewish parents
both of whom were descended from well-known rabbis.
His father, a lawyer, had become a Protestant Christian
in 1817, in order to avoid the disabilities then being
placed on Jews in Germany. Karl Marx went in 1835 to
the University of Bonn to study law, and in 1836 to
Berlin where, after a further period working at law he
turned over to philosophy in spite of his father's en-
deavours to persuade him to continue with a course that
would have prepared him for a safe career. What
fascinated Marx about philosophy was the controversy
going on about the views of Hegel who had been professor
of philosophy at Berlin from 1818 until his death in 1832.
Hegel had developed an elaborate and comprehensive
system of thought in which he appeared to argue that
mind and spirit are fundamental in the universe, that
Christianity expresses in pictorial form the absolute
truth about God and man, and that human history is a
progress towards rational freedom that takes place,
however, by means of dialectical oppositions and struggles
rather than by gradual stages. Hegel's most influential
followers regarded him as a defender of Christianity and
of a moderate political conservatism, but others, known
as "Young Hegelians", accentuated his account of
dialectical opposition and used it to arrive at radical
views in politics and religion. Marx attached himself to
this latter group and at one time hoped to become a
university teacher of philosophy. Having been convinced,
however, that his political views would make this impossible, he began his literary career as editor of the
Rheinische Zeitung in 1842. He vigorously defended the

freedom of the press against those who believed that subversive religious and philosophical views should be kept from publication, but in 1843 the Prussian government suppressed the paper as a result of complaints from the Tsar of Russia who resented attacks on him that had been printed in it.

So in November 1843 Marx went to Paris to collaborate in a new journal, the *Deutsch-Französische Jahrbücher*. Attempts were made to get contributions from various distinguished French authors. The Catholic social reformer Lammenais was approached, but was unwilling to contribute to a journal which he rightly suspected would be hostile to Christianity. The French socialist Louis Blanc also refused, for somewhat similar reasons, as did the poet Lamartine, for whom the journal's aims were far too revolutionary. In the event only one issue of the journal appeared, in March 1844, and there were no French contributors. Marx himself provided two articles, one *On the Jewish Question*, and the other on Hegel's *Philosophy of Right*. It is in the latter article that Marx described religion as "the opium of the people". The poet, Heinrich Heine, contributed some poems that mocked King Ludwig of Bavaria, and there were two articles by Friedrich Engels. One of these, entitled "The Condition of England", was a detailed discussion of Thomas Carlyle's *Past and Present*, which had appeared in 1843. The other, entitled *Sketch of a Critique of Political Economy*, is a remarkable first sketch of what was later to be called Marxist socialism, and one can say, with only very slight exaggeration, that Engels was the first exponent of the view. In the autumn of 1844 Engels came to Paris and a lifelong partnership began.

Engels' career had been less academic than that of
Marx. He was born at Barmen in 1820, the son of a
prosperous textile manufacturer. At the age of seventeen
he entered his father's business and in the following year
went to learn commerce with a friend of his father who
had an export textile business at Bremen. But Engels
did not give all his time to commerce. He wrote poetry,
and during 1839 started contributing articles to various
newspapers. During the same year he read David
Strauss' *Life of Jesus* (1835) and was led by it to become
an atheist. Strauss was one of those who had been
influenced by Hegel but drew revolutionary conclusions
about religion from their study of his writings, and so
Engels began to move in a similar direction to that being
taken, quite independently, by Marx. Engels arranged to
do his military service in Berlin where he made the
acquaintance of some of the "Young Hegelians" and
attended a course of lectures in defence of the Christian
revelation given by the famous anti-Hegelian philosopher
Schelling. In 1842 Engels published two pamphlets
attacking these lectures and towards the end of the year
he went to Manchester to work in a textile firm in which
his father had a financial interest. In England Engels got
to know some leading Chartists and contributed to Feargus
O'Connor's journal, *The Northern Star*, as well as to
Robert Owen's *The New Moral World*. Engels' journal-
istic activities from 1843 to 1845 consisted in sending
articles about Chartism and the English working class to
papers on the Continent and articles about continental
socialism to the English Chartist papers. When Engels
began to work with Marx in 1844 he knew much
more about economics and about industrial and social

conditions than Marx did and brought to the partnership a knowledge that was indispensible to its success.⁵

In *The German Ideology*, the unpublished joint work to which we have already referred, the central Marxist doctrine, that was subsequently called Historical Materialism, was developed in some detail. Marx himself gave another brief account of it in *The Poverty of Philosophy* (1847), written in criticism of a book called *The Philosophy of Poverty* by the French socialist, Proudhon. By this time Marx and Engels were both active among socialists and working-class organizations, and when a body known as the Communist League, with members in Paris, Brussels and London was founded in 1847, it was decided that a statement of its principles should be drawn up. The London Committee wrote to Marx, who had had to leave Paris for Brussels, asking him to do this. Engels had suggested to him the title "Communist Manifesto" and had given Marx a catechism of communist ideas and proposals, but Marx worked this up into a more eloquent and forceful version which was published as their joint work in German in London in February 1848.⁶ It appeared in French in Paris before the Revolution of 1848 and an English version was published in 1850 in *The Red Republican*, a paper edited by George Harney. Harney was one of those Chartists who believed in insurrectionary violence and were hence called "physical force" Chartists. *The Communist Manifesto* stated that all history hitherto had been a history of class struggles, that the bourgeoisie, having ousted the feudal aristocracy, were now confronted by the proletariat, that the proletariat was now the only revolutionary class and that the communists, with their demand for the abolition of private

property, would lead the proletariat to victory over
the bourgeoisie and to the formation of a society free
from class antagonisms "in which the free development of each is the condition for the free development
of all". The *Manifesto* ended with these ominous
words:

The Communists disdain to conceal their views and aims.
They openly declare that their ends can be attained only
by the forcible overthrow of all existing social conditions.
Let the ruling classes tremble at a communist revolution.
The proletarians have nothing to lose but their chains.
They have a world to gain. Working men of all countries,
unite!

§2 *The Eighteen-forties*

By the eighteen-forties, when Marx and Engels began
their joint career, industrial capitalism was developing
fast. Most of the early factories had been built in the
countryside but by the eighteen-forties they were being
concentrated in large towns, and large populations were
growing up in places like Roubaix in France and Manchester in England. Railways were spreading all over
western Europe, extending the market for what the
factories produced and making it easier for people to
change their place of work. Some men became very rich
in organizing all this, some gained fortunes and lost them
again, many found they could not continue at their old
crafts and had to search for jobs in the factory towns.
In the factories the discipline was often strict and the
hours worked very long. Furthermore, employers and
governments tended to regard associations of workmen
as conspiracies, so that strike leaders were often deported

or imprisoned. It had become apparent well before the eighteen-forties that industrial development was not taking place in an orderly and steady way, but spurts of activity with high profits and increased wages were succeeded by slumps when fortunes were lost, thousands became unemployed and wages dropped. Working men who had lived through the period called it later on "the hungry forties", for little had been done to help those who fell out of work through no fault of their own. In *Past and Present* (1843) Carlyle tells of a widow who failed to obtain relief and in the course of trying to get help, infected seventeen people with typhus fever of which they died. He writes, too, of parents who poisoned three of their children to defraud a burial society of £3. 8s. Engels, in his *Condition of the Working Class in England* (1845), describes the miseries of the workers in the new factory towns more coherently though no less indignantly than Carlyle.

The eighteen-forties was a period of political unrest too. In England the Chartists were putting forward demands for manhood suffrage and annual parliaments; in Germany, as we have seen, there was press censorship in defence of the monarchy and the Church; and in France under Louis-Philippe it was said that society was "dancing the polka on a volcano". The volcano erupted in 1848 when the French monarchy was swept away. But in Germany the revolution collapsed in ignominy. Engels was one of the few who actually took up arms against the government. In England, too, there were riots and conspiracies, but Chartism was defeated, and it was left to a conservative, Disraeli, to make the next moves towards the enfranchisement of the working classes nearly twenty years later. It became clear in the eighteen-forties, however, that "the masses", as the "Young Hegelians" called the working classes, or the proletariat, as Marx and Engels called them, were becoming a force to be reckoned with in capitalist society. Priests like Lamennais and Frederic Denison Maurice and novelists like Georges Sand and Eugène Sue were calling attention to the plight of the proletariat. Marx and Engels did so too, but believed that the proletariat could not be succoured from without but would so assert itself as to become identical with the whole of mankind. They therefore decided to provide it with a faith and with a leadership.

§3   Laissez-faire *Liberalism*

In the seventeenth and eighteenth centuries the governments of Europe pursued policies of state control over trade and commerce with the aim of strengthening national power and national wealth. Governments forbade the emigration of skilled workmen, placed tariffs on imports, granted monopolies to trading companies, fixed wages and prices and enforced systems of apprenticeship, subsidized the building of merchant ships and carried out many other policies of control in pursuit of national wealth and aggrandizement. These networks of controls and regulations often hampered trade and discouraged industry, and in eighteenth-century France a number of able writers urged that they should be removed. These critics of Mercantilism, as the system of state control has since been called, named their system of economic thought "Physiocracy", using this word to emphasize their belief in a spontaneous and natural economic order (the Greek word *physis* meaning "nature") as opposed to the regulated one that then prevailed. One of these Physiocrats expressed their demand for a policy of economic freedom in the words: *"Laissez faire, laissez passer, le monde va de lui-même"* ("Let people produce, let them move about freely, the world goes on its own").

Now Adam Smith's *Wealth of Nations* (1776) is generally regarded as the foundation of classical political economy. A large part of this book is a detailed criticism of the mercantilist system, and although Adam Smith rejected some of the physiocrats' theories he concluded that national wealth would be much increased by adopting the natural or free system of commerce and industry. He argued that monopolies and tariffs sheltered the inefficient, that individuals were more likely than governments to recognize and seize opportunities for new forms of trade and production, and that the self-interest of business men could be relied upon in most cases to promote the production and sale of the goods that consumers need. He believed, too, that Mercantilism favoured producers at the expense of consumers, and he argued that competition between producers and between merchants benefited the community as a whole.

In the generation after Adam Smith's death, his views were developed and elaborated so as to provide a sort of moral defence of the capitalist system as it was then emerging. Smith himself had shown little admiration for business men, whom he suspected of being only too ready to conspire against the public. His plea for free and spontaneous economic activity, however, was welcomed by those who were setting up new firms and industries and wished to break free from the restrictions which the now conservative agricultural interests were anxious to retain. It thus came about that the *laissez-faire* economic outlook was adopted by middle-class business men who were irked by controls maintained by the land-owning aristocracy. These middle-class business men and industrialists were employers of labour, and they opposed combinations among workmen, just as they opposed privileged monopolies and restrictions upon trade. Writers on economics told them that trade-union pressure to put up the wages of one group of workmen would only lead to lower wages for other groups. Some economists argued, too, that legislation to shorten the working day or to produce safety and cleanliness in factories, would prove crippling to the industry on which it was imposed. Others said that public assistance to the poor and even private charity were dangerous to the working of the competitive system. Employers of labour were regarded by some as benevolent abstainers from immediate enjoyment who, as a result of their laudable sacrifices in the form of savings, were able to provide wage-earners with the opportunity to live and work and earn.

Such views as these did not go unopposed. Sismondi (1773–1842) suggested in 1819 that unless steps were taken to correct it, the competitive system tended to bring about economic crises and unemployment as the result of there not being enough money in the hands of the working population to enable them to buy all the goods produced. Sismondi proposed that this overproduction (or underconsumption) should be dealt with, not by reducing production but by raising wages to a level that would make it possible for the wage-earners to buy all the goods they produced. Malthus, one of the classical economists, gave an analysis of the same predicament of underconsumption in 1836, arguing that there was a tendency for the savings of business men so to increase the amount of capital that there was insufficient demand to buy the goods that the increased capital was responsible for producing. Malthus saw that it might be possible to remedy this by issuing more money, but such an inflationary policy, he thought, would be unjust. Instead he recommended that in periods of inadequate demand, schemes of public works should be instituted to provide employment for those thrown out of work. Thomas Carlyle was another critic of extreme *laissez-faire*, but his criticisms were political rather than economic. In *Chartism* (1839) he wrote that *laissez-faire* is "an abdication on the part of governors" and jibed at the "Paralytic Radicalism" which teaches that "nothing whatever can be done in it by the wit of man who has simply to sit still and look wistfully to 'time and general laws'." Carlyle believed that if governments did not intervene to bring economic affairs under control there would be a collapse of authority and a revolution of the masses.

Engels' *Sketch of a Critique of Political Economy* of 1844—it was written in 1843—therefore, important as it was for its influence on Marx's views, was by no means an isolated criticism of the *laissez-faire* outlook. Sismondi and Malthus, however, like Keynes in our own day, had suggested ways in which a predominantly competitive capitalism could be made to work, whereas Engels argued that competitive capitalism was bound to result in new forms of monopoly that would bring about its own downfall. Addressing the supporters of the free enterprise system, Engels writes:

You have destroyed the small monopolies so that the *one* great basic monopoly, property, may function the more freely and unrestrictedly; you have civilized the ends of the earth to win new terrain for the unfolding of your low avarice; you have made all men brothers, but it is a brotherhood of thieves. [9]

In this passage Engels is saying that the advances in invention and production brought about under the system of competitive capitalism have been at the behest of greed and have spread greed among men. But Engels also believed that out of all this a new society would be born, so that the capitalist and his supporting economists were unwittingly helping in the development of a new social order. [10]

But the economist does not know himself what cause he serves. He does not know that with all his egoistical reasoning he nevertheless forms but a link in the chain of mankind's universal progress. He does not know that by his dissolution of all sectional interests he merely paves the way for the great transformation to which the century is moving, the reconciliation of mankind with nature and itself. [11]

Out of the crises, monopolies and revolutions to which the free enterprise system will give rise will emerge a form of society in which men associate and combine in order to produce for themselves the goods which they need. [12]

If the producers as such knew how much the consumers required, if they were to organize production, if they were to share it out amongst themselves, then the fluctuations of competition and its tendency to crisis would be impossible. Produce with consciousness as human beings—not as dispersed atoms without consciousness of your kind, and you are beyond all these artificial and untenable antitheses. [13]

§4 *Pre-Marxist Socialism*

In the above-quoted passages from Engels' essay, we may notice that he criticizes the competitive system on moral and economic grounds. He says, in the first place, that it is a system based on greed, yet he also says that it is a system that is bound to destroy itself. But out of this destruction something better is to emerge, a system in which goods are co-operatively produced in accordance with a plan and distributed to those who need them. His central idea is that a spontaneous and allegedly chaotic economic order should and will be replaced by an order in which production and distribution are planned for society as a whole. This, of course, is the central idea of socialism. We have seen that in the eighteen-forties Marx and Engels were active among socialist groups in Paris, Brussels, Manchester and London. Their relations with these groups, however, were by no means harmonious. Marx's *Poverty of Philosophy* was an attack on the views of the French socialist, Proudhon (whom Marx regarded as a petit-bourgeois rather than as a supporter of the proletarian cause). In the unpublished *German Ideology* various German socialists had been attacked. In *The Communist Manifesto* several pages are devoted to attacks on forms of socialism that Marx found unacceptable. For example, Christian Socialism was ridiculed as:

The holy water with which the priest consecrates the spite of the aristocrat. [5]

In the same work, Marx refers to what he calls "critical-Utopian socialism", and mentions Saint-Simon, Owen and Fourier. He praises these socialists for their criticisms of capitalist society, but condemns them for their failure to provide political leadership for the working classes. What then, did Marx and Engels accept and what did they reject from the socialist views already in existence?

We need not at present consider Saint-Simon. Robert Owen (1771–1858) and François-Marie Charles Fourier (1772–1837) may be described as advocates of voluntary socialism. That is, they looked forward to the establishment of planned and organized non-capitalistic societies by men and women who had withdrawn from capitalist society to form for themselves a non-competitive, harmonious, co-operative social order. Owen tried to interest leading statesmen and even royalty in his schemes, and Fourier waited at a fixed time every day for the wealthy backer who never came. Owen himself founded a community called New Harmony in Indiana (then a frontier area), and some of Fourier's disciples set up "phalansteries", as they were called, in other parts of the United States. None of these communities persisted for very long in their original form, although some lasted to the end of the nineteenth century as somewhat unusual types of industrial companies. The failure of Owen's experiment at New Harmony was apparent long before Marx and Engels became socialists. Now although Owen was an opponent of Christianity, and although Fourier's advocacy of sexual experiment and variety went against Christian teaching, the Owenite and Fourierist communities had something in common with such religious sects as the Shakers and Rappists which had established themselves in the United States in the eighteenth century. Indeed, socialist communities sometimes established themselves in settlements abandoned by such bodies. These voluntary socialists abandoned "the world" and endeavoured to pursue a new way of life devoted to ideals of brotherliness and love. They were a sort of secular church withdrawn from the trading and huckstering which deformed life in the capitalist world.

In marked contrast to these pacific forms of socialism were those that traced their origin back to the French Revolution of 1789. That revolution was, of course, in its main developments a revolution of the peasants and middle-classes against the aristocracy. It was, however, a revolution which proceeded by means of insurrection, terror and violence, and in the course of it necessity and perhaps some popular pressures brought about rationing and price control. With the fall of Robespierre and the Jacobins in 1794, however, the Revolution took on a more conservative form. But in 1796 Baboeuf and some other socialists joined with a group of disgruntled Jacobins and some disaffected army men in a conspiracy to set up a dictatorial government that would have enforced the nationalization of the land and of industry and then would have introduced a democratic constitution to ratify and continue these socialist measures. The plot was betrayed and Baboeuf went to the guillotine. One of the leading conspirators, Buonarotti (1761–1838), a descendant of Michelangelo, was deported and then released. He settled in Belgium where he wrote an account of the movement and of its aims. This was published in 1828 and provided inspiration for socialists who took part in the French Revolutions of 1830 and 1848. It was translated into English by the Chartist leader, Bronterre O'Brien, in 1838. One of O'Brien's associates, George Harney, the "physical force" Chartist we have already referred to, was much impressed by this and by the French revolutionary literature, and affected a style of Jacobin journalism in some of his articles in Chartist newspapers. Engels knew O'Brien and Harney and also members of a body known as the League of the Just who continued to uphold Baboeuf's insurrectionary tradition. Marx knew them too, and, with Engels, wrote *The Communist Manifesto* at the request of the Communist League, a body with a similar outlook. We have already seen that the first English translation of *The Communist Manifesto* was published in Harney's *The Red Republican.*

Marx was undoubtedly impressed by this insurrectionary tradition. His surviving notebooks show that he made a close study of the French Revolution. He thought that the peasant and middle-class revolution succeeded because the time was ripe for it, and that Baboeuf's plot failed because it was premature. He thought, too, that it was unrealistic of Owen and of Fourier to expect men of wealth to support them in schemes whose outcome, if successful, would be a form of society in which there would be no aristocracy and no capitalists. Successful revolutions are brought about by those who have an interest in their success. The French peasants and bourgeoisie of the eighteenth century had an interest in not being mulcted for the benefit of the aristocracy, and so they took forcible steps to dispossess them. A new class of wage-earners or proletarians was being formed and exploited by the growth of capitalist industry. A revolution that favoured their interests was bound to succeed if the system of capitalist competition was inherently unstable as Engels said it was.

2   Marxist Materialism

§1   *Hegelian Philosophy and Feuerbach's Criticism of It*

We have seen that while Marx was a university student he turned from the study of law to the study of philosophy and soon became involved in the current controversies about the philosophy of Hegel. Hegel is described in the textbooks as an idealist, but this term does not greatly help in understanding his complex and comprehensive system. Perhaps the fundamental feature of Hegel's philosophy was its opposition to materialism and to empiricism, two points of view which had been widely held in the eighteenth century. Materialism is the view that nothing is real but what is material and that minds must therefore be forms of matter. Empiricism is the view that knowledge is based on sense experience and that thought and reasoning cannot be anything but elaborations of sense experience; a French writer, Destutt de Tracy, had summarized this latter theory in the phrase:

"penser, c'est sentir". At the very end of the eighteenth century a number of German philosophers criticized both materialism and empiricism, holding that they were inconsistent with the very possibility of scientific reasoning and human freedom. Indications of this line of thought are found in some of the writings of Kant (1724–1804), but it was pursued in a more positive way by Fichte (1762–1814), Schelling (1775–1854) and Hegel (1770–1831). It is interesting to notice that the English poet and writer, Samuel Taylor Coleridge, was greatly impressed by Kant's and Schelling's writings, some ideas from which he utilized in formulating his views on poetry. These German idealists claimed to show that thought and freedom are inseparable, that is, that no being could think and reason unless it had will and freedom. It was Hegel who gave the most elaborate exposition of this point of view. The first part of his system was concerned with logic, by which he meant the concepts in terms of which the world is understood. The second part was the philosophy of nature and the third part the philosophy of mind. It seemed to his contemporaries that Hegel believed he could somehow derive or deduce the philosophy of nature from the logic and the philosophy of mind from the two preceding parts. It certainly was his view that the very concepts used by materialists and empiricists, such concepts as number, shape, quantity, space, movement, are unstable and contradictory and lead on to more adequate concepts that culminate in those of mind, society, art, religion and, in the end, philosophy.

It was an important idea in Hegel's philosophy that specialists in the sciences, such as mathematicians, chemists and biologists, carry on their researches without asking questions about their own fundamental assumptions. Mathematicians do not ask what numbers are, chemists do not question the notion of interacting substances, biologists write about animal species and about life itself as if these ideas are in no need of examination. But it is the task of philosophy, according to Hegel, to subject these and cognate conceptions to critical scrutiny, and to show how they are related to mind and thought, to human society, and to art, religion and philosophy itself. Thus Hegel believed that any account of man and of his place in the world that took the material world and ordinary sense experience for granted was bound to be superficial and inadequate. The last word on ultimate problems, he held, must be uttered by the philosopher. Hegel called this ultimate and authoritative philosophical task Speculative Philosophy. In using the adjective "speculative" he did not mean to imply that philosophy proceeds by hunch or by guess, like speculators in risky shares, but rather that it goes beyond anything that sense experience and scientific enquiry could establish (Kant had used the word in this way previously). According to Hegel, then, Speculative Philosophy shows the limitations of the concepts of scientific specialists; shows, too, that the concepts of mind, of freedom and of social life are less inadequate, leading on to art, religion and philosophy. It will be noticed that in Hegel's system religious concepts are thought to bring us very close to the ultimate truth of things. Their defect, according to Hegel, is that they express the ultimate truth in imaginative or pictorial forms. Genuine philosophical thinking, he held, takes us beyond pictures and images to a self-conscious grasp of what is ultimate, the absolute mind.

Views somewhat similar in scope had been put forward before Hegel, by Leibniz (1646–1716), for example, and they were revived later in the nineteenth century by philosophers who are known as neo-Hegelians. These ideas have an intellectual and human appeal, which makes it unlikely that they will never be revived again. Hegel's version of this type of philosophy, however, was published at a time when natural science was advancing very rapidly and was beginning to claim an intellectual superiority over theology and philosophy. In France, in the eighteen-twenties and thirties Auguste Comte (1798–1857) was already advocating Positivism, the view that human knowledge can *only* be obtained by using the methods of the natural sciences. If Comte and the Positivists were right, then Hegel's Speculative Philosophy was an immense and pretentious mistake. In Germany in the late eighteen-thirties and early eighteen-forties Ludwig Feuerbach (1804–72) was coming to a similar conclusion. He had attended Hegel's lectures and had started by accepting his main views. But in 1839 he published a *Critique of the Hegelian Philosophy* to show how fundamentally unsound they are. One of his criticisms was that what Hegel thought was a proof or demonstration of his system was really nothing but a statement of it, since Hegel assumed throughout the truth of the conclusions he sought to establish. Hence, instead of showing what is the case, Hegel was arbitrarily elaborating concepts of his own choosing. Feuerbach also objected that Hegel was seriously at fault in his account of nature. As we have seen, Hegel seems to have held that nature somehow emerges out of thought and the categories of logic. Feuerbach asserted, however, that the very idea of nature

involves the sense experiences of creatures possessing sense organs and therefore bodies. We get to know nature by seeing and touching and hearing, and would not do these things without eyes and hands and ears. This being so, men and their thoughts must be regarded as parts of nature. Feuerbach did not say that thoughts are nothing but movements of material things (though he did say that "man is what he eats"), but he argued that thinking should be regarded as something that human beings *do*, and that they are creatures with sense organs and brains, parts and products of the natural world. It was Feuerbach's view that Hegel had lost sight of these fundamental facts and had hence come to regard thought and thinking in an unrealistic way. Thought, according to Feuerbach, arises within nature and cannot rightly be supposed to be beyond or above it.

In the *Essence of Christianity* (1841) Feuerbach applied these ideas to Christianity. We do not see or hear or smell God, nor have we such evidence for his existence as we have for stars or atoms. Nor can we go to heaven or hell and report upon them on our return. Our thoughts about these subjects, therefore, must have arisen from our human nature and from the human situation. We have never met an infinitely powerful and loving being, and hence our idea of God as such a being must be a human creation based on our knowledge of human power and human goodness. God, according to Feuerbach, is a projection of the highest qualities that exist among men, and a fusing of them together in an imaginary being. In worshipping God, men unwittingly elaborate human perfection, and in yearning after Him, they unwittingly yearn after what they hope to be. "God", says Feuerbach in a phrase that stuck in Marx's mind and was echoed in a passage we shall soon be examining, is an "inexpressible sigh deep in the souls of men". In heaven the good are rewarded and in hell the bad are punished, and justice is secured thereby. But according to Feuerbach, heaven and hell are imaginary places and the justice secured in them is an imaginary justice. In the real world things do not always work out this way, and it is *because* they cannot secure justice on earth that men imagine its achievement elsewhere. Feuerbach believed that if justice reigned on earth, a supernatural mechanism for obtaining heavenly substitutes for it would be superfluous. Men fail to fulfil themselves in their earthly lives, the only lives they have, and compensate for this by imagining supernatural fulfilments. They do not do this wittingly, but if they become conscious of what they are doing, they would turn from fantasies to earthly things.

In books that were published soon after the *Essence of Christianity*, Feuerbach argued that theology is empty theorizing about religion and that Speculative Philosophy is theology in disguise. Once theologians and philosophers became conscious of this, they would cease to engage in these fruitless activities and would start studying man and his real earthly problems instead. "The mystery of theology," Feuerbach wrote, "is anthropology." By "anthropology" he meant what today we call psychology and sociology. So what he meant by this phrase was that if we came to understand what men are doing when they construct theological systems or engage in Speculative Philosophy, we should turn our attention to human beings, their motives, aims and social organizations. Theology and Speculative Philosophy would then be, so to say, *explained away*, for no one would wittingly chase will-o'-the-wisps.

Feuerbach's general philosophical view may be described as materialism, and Marx and Engels regarded it as such. But it is not the sort of materialism that reduces thoughts to brain events or to atomic or sub-atomic transformations. It is the sort of materialism according to which thoughts are human activities, human beings are parts of nature, and nature is something which has developed on its own, without creation or pre-ordained plan. Feuerbach's materialism is a sort of inversion of Hegel's idealism. According to Hegel the doctrines of the Christian religion take us very close to a knowledge of reality, and Speculative Philosophy gives this knowledge its ultimate rational form, whereas sense knowledge and the sciences based upon it reveal only superficial aspects of the world. But according to Feuerbach it is sense experience and the special sciences which reveal the world as it is, while theology and Speculative Philosophy mislead their practitioners and should be regarded as expressions of hopes and wishes rather than as knowledge of things as they are. In the *Essence of Christianity* Feuerbach regarded the various Christian dogmas as signs that need interpretation, as indications, not of a supernatural world, but of human aims and hopes that are denied fulfilment. He instituted a practice that has been widely adopted since he wrote, of treating what people say as an unwitting revelation of what they do not say. One development of this method is the Freudian practice of regarding dreams, slips of the tongue and even some deliberate utterances as symptoms of underlying wants. Another is the Marxist practice of rejecting the overt meaning of economic or political theories and of interpreting them as disguises for class interests. Both Freud's method of seeking for the latent or hidden content of dreams behind their manifest content, and Marx's method of "unmasking" the class interests concealed behind the words of social and political theorists, owe their origin to Feuerbach's revelation, as he put it, of the "mystery of theology". It was he who first claimed that suitably trained observers, skilled in interpreting signs and symptoms, could understand people better than they understand themselves.

§2 *"Religion is the opium of the people"*

Marx's contribution to the *Deutsch-Französische Jahrbücher* of 1844, *Towards a Critique of the Hegelian Theory of Law: Introduction*, was written under the influence of Feuerbach's *Essence of Christianity*, and, indeed, is in large part an exposition of Feuerbach's views. This can be shown if we consider the whole passage, near the beginning of the article, in which the phrase, "Religion is the opium of the people", occurs. The third, fourth and fifth paragraphs of Marx's essay are as follows:

The basis of irreligious criticism is: *Man makes religion,* religion does not make man. Religion is indeed the self-consciousness and self-feeling of man who has not yet gained possession of himself or has already lost himself again. But man is not an abstract being lurking outside the world. *Man is the world of men,* state, society. This state, this society produces religion, *an inverted consciousness of the world,* because it is *an inverted world.* Religion is the general theory of this world, its encyclopædic compendium, its logic in popular form, its spiritual point

d'honneur, its enthusiasm, its moral sanction, its ceremonial enhancement, its general ground for justification and consolation. Religion is the realization of the essence of man in the imagination because the essence of man has no true realization. The battle against religion is thus indirectly the battle against that world whose spiritual aroma religion is.

Religious want is both the expression of real want and the protest against real want. Religion is the sigh of the oppressed creature, the heart of a heartless world, the soul of soulless circumstances. It is the opium of the people.

To remove religion as the people's illusory happiness is to demand real happiness for the people. The demand for the abandonment of illusions about one's condition is *the demand to give up a condition that needs illusion.* The criticism of religion is thus in embryo the criticism of the vale of sorrows whose halo is religion.

There are several important points we should notice here. In the first place it is clear that Marx, like Feuerbach, regarded religion as something produced by man himself. Marx held, that is, that religion is a natural phenomenon that arises in human societies, and is not, as religious people themselves believe, an opening into a world beyond nature and superior to it. Once this is granted— and many of course would refuse to grant it—then the question that needs to be answered is: *How* does human society give rise to religion? The answer that Marx, again following Feuerbach, gives to this question is that human society is so constituted that most men are in want and human nature is frustrated, is unable to achieve all it might achieve, cannot realize its true nature or

essence. Since men cannot satisfy their wants or overcome their frustrations in society as it is, in "this vale of
sorrows", they imagine another world beyond in which all
their wants are satisfied, ruled over by a Being in whom is
realized man's supreme potentialities. In this way they
are consoled for their present unhappiness and are
enabled to justify its continuance. If they could not do
this they would find the unhappiness of the world un-
bearable. The religious view of things is an inverted
image of the real world (the phrase "inverted world" is
from Hegel), in the sense that whereas in the real world
there is unhappiness, in the imagined supernatural world
there is happiness, and whereas in the real world there is
failure, in the inverted image there is success. If, therefore,
we investigate the religion of a people we are not really
exploring a world beyond this world, but are examining
symptoms that reveal the social diseases from which the
people are suffering.

What, then, does Marx think is the remedy for the
religious illusion? Feuerbach devoted much of his life
to the task of explaining what the religious illusion is and
how it arises, so that men who accepted his views might,
to use his own expression, become "disillusioned" about
it. He had also said that the need for religious illusions
would be lessened if social conditions were improved. He
actually wrote: "Let politics become our religion", a
demand which has been fulfilled in the twentieth century
in ways with which we are only too familiar. This last
was the course that Marx advocated when he said that the
demand to abandon illusions about the human condition
was "the demand to give up a condition that needs
illusion". In a "heartless world" men must seek for

consolation beyond the world. Men suffering under oppression that they see no means of getting free from, sigh for release, and their sigh is religion. Religion brings them temporary relief, as opium brings relief to the poor and hopeless. But just as it is better to face the world rather than to escape into opium dreams, so it is better to reform society than to take refuge from it in an imaginary supernatural kingdom.

Marx does not mean that priests are necessarily impostors who cunningly divert the workers' attention from their grievances by telling them lies about God and a spiritual world. Still less does he mean that men could be "cured" of their religious beliefs by proving them false, as men might possibly be cured of drug addiction by lectures about the injury it does to them. The central idea is that religion is a social and psychological mechanism that makes the lives of unhappy men bearable to themselves and serves as a justification for the sufferings they undergo. It is, indeed, symptomatic of these sufferings. The sufferings themselves are due to social maladjustments, and if these were remedied, religion would lose its *raison d'être* and cease to exist. Attacks on religion are indirectly attacks on the evils of society. Attacks on the evils of society are indirectly attacks on religion. Social revolution is therefore essentially anti-Christian and irreligious, since if successful it would abolish the conditions in which religion arises. It is not surprising that, accepting these views about religion and society, Marx and Engels believed that socialism and irreligion go together. What is surprising is that any Christian could ever have thought that Christianity and Marxism are reconcilable.

§3 *Changing the World*

In the article we have been discussing, Marx maintained that philosophy must henceforth be practical. On this Marx differed from Hegel who, in his *Philosophy of Right*, had said that history cannot be rejuvenated by philosophy but may only be understood by it. Although Marx rejected Speculative Philosophy, he considered that this very rejection must ensure that critical philosophy or philosophical criticism becomes an agency of social change. For the philosophical critic is necessarily an opponent of religion and of its associated phantasies, and in opposing these things he comes into opposition with the real world that gave rise to them. To criticize religion effectively, it is necessary to transform society. Marx put this by saying that philosophy is bound up with *Praxis*. (This word, which has been repeatedly used by Marx's followers, was borrowed by Marx from a book entitled *Prolegomena zur Historiosophie* (1838) by A. von Cieszkowski (1814–94), who held that Hegel was wrong in regarding philosophy as interpreting the past rather than as making the future. Cieszkowski used the word "Praxis" for the practical effect which he thought philosophy should have, and wrote that philosophy should influence the life of men "not only in present reality, but in the more developed reality of the future".) But practice, if it is to be effective, must, Marx held, utilize the proper means, and when practice is directed towards social change it must utilize whatever favourable social forces there are available. Marx believed that the revolutionary force in capitalist society is the proletariat, the men and women who have to earn wages in order to live. In capitalist society this class is deprived and depressed but if it were properly led, Marx believed, it could free itself and in doing so free mankind as a whole. The emancipation of the proletariat would become the emancipation of mankind. Marx rhetorically concluded:

The head of this emancipation is philosophy, its heart the proletariat. Philosophy cannot realize itself without an uprising of the proletariat, and the proletariat cannot raise itself up without the realization of philosophy.

Various themes and arguments converge in this passage, which is the first indication of the doctrinally united revolutionary party that Marx and Engels always worked for. Philosophers who recognize the importance of sense experience and who regard the methods of the natural sciences as paramount, Marx is arguing, oppose the whole idea of seeking the illusory and imaginative satisfactions which are all that religion can provide. They understand why these illusory substitute satisfactions have been sought, and they then ascertain how genuine satisfactions can be obtained here on earth. Finding that the proletariat are the chief victims of the capitalist system, the philosophers conclude that the proletariat must have strong motives for overthrowing it. This is what Marx means when he says that the proletariat is "the heart" of emancipation. The overthrow of capitalism is something that must be close to the hearts of the proletariat. The philosopher, therefore, helps the proletariat by providing it with leadership and a doctrine, which Marx calls its "head". Correct philosophical doctrine, consciously pursued opposition to religion, and efficacious social revolution are clearly associated with one another. True social understanding and realistically undertaken social revolution are inseparable. Marx expressed this view a year later in some notes about Feuerbach which Engels discovered and published in 1886, one of which reads:

The philosophers have only *interpreted* the world differently, the point is to change it.

§4 *Main Features of Marx's Materialism*

(*a*) Marx passionately rejected all forms of supernaturalism. That is, he rejected all views, whether couched in religious or in philosophical terms, which attempt to explain man and nature as products or manifestations of a mind that transcends nature. Thus his view is a species of *Naturalism*.

(*b*) Marx thought that human knowledge must be based upon sense experience, and thus his view is a species of *Empiricism*. It is because he is an empiricist that he is a naturalist.

(*c*) Marx rejected the claims of Speculative Philosophers (to use his expression) or of metaphysicians (to use the term current today) to obtain knowledge of the world other than the knowledge obtained by use of the scientific methods. This view, that the only knowledge of the world is that obtained by the special sciences such as physics, chemistry or biology, is called *Positivism*. Marx was undoubtedly a positivist, although he would not have called himself by that name, as he disliked many of the social views of Comte, the leading positivist of the nineteenth century.

(*d*) Marx (like Feuerbach) believed that religious beliefs and practices do not have the significance that their adherents think they have. He held, rather, that they must be explained in natural terms, and that these natural terms are psychological and social. That is, Marx was an *atheist*.

(*e*) Marx believed that philosophical and scientific knowledge are inherently practical. The view that knowledge is essentially practical is today called *Pragmatism*, and pragmatism is undoubtedly an aspect of Marx's materialism.

Marx's materialism, then, is a combination of naturalism, empiricism, positivism, atheism and pragmatism. But even these descriptions do not exhaust the complexity of his materialist view, for Marx also considered that his materialism was "dialectical". The expression "dialectical materialism" is not used either by Marx or by Engels, but was invented by the Russian Marxist, Plekhanov (1856–1918). It is therefore anachronistic to apply it to Marx's own theories. Nevertheless, Marx regarded its dialectical character as one of the merits of Hegel's philosophy which he had incorporated into his own. But as his main concern with dialectics was in his account of society and of history, we can defer discussion of this topic until the next chapter.

3 Historical Materialism

§1 *Philosophies of History*

Even the most savage peoples have some interest in their
ancestors and in the origins of their society. More
civilized peoples look back to such heroes as Abraham
and Aeneas, and sometimes imagine a Golden Age before
men were corrupted by lust and greed. Religious teachers
have contrasted the benighted condition of the world
before its saviour came with the enlightenment that
followed His arrival. In Christianity a line is drawn
between the period before Christ's coming and the era
when the Church is spreading His influence in the world.
Christians look forward, too, to the end of history, when
all men will be judged. Thus myth and religion provide
various simple schemes for introducing an order into the
human past and for showing the present generation its
place in history.

About the seventeenth century, however, a major new concern was introduced into human life, experimental science. Once this was well established, it provided a new principle of historical order, for it enabled men to look at the past as a gradual advance in invention and scientific understanding. Thus, at the end of the eighteenth century, Condorcet (1743–94) conceived of human history as a growth in human knowledge or enlightenment. Condorcet was a leading figure in the French Revolution, and like others among his revolutionary associates, he believed that mankind was at that time moving into a new epoch. In the past men had been subjected to a nature they did not understand and to rules they could not control, but by breaking the power of priests and kings and by taking their lives into their own hands, men would recreate society and themselves. Scientific advance, it was thought, opened the way for indefinite moral improvement.

Two branches of knowledge that were being created at the beginning of the nineteenth century encouraged the growing tendency to divide up the past into epochs. One of these was geology, or geognosis, as it was first called. Earlier generations had thought that the earth and the animal species on it were created all at once. But examination of rocks and fossils was making it pretty clear that the earth had passed through various phases of development and that different sorts of animals had inhabited the earth during the periods when it was possible for each species to keep alive. Archaeology was also presenting reasons for believing that the earliest men had been able to use only weapons and tools made of stone, and that later on they learned the use of iron and bronze.

Hence prehistoric society was divided into a Stone Age
and an Iron Age, on the basis of the tools that men had
invented and had come to utilize. About the same time
there was much speculation about the historical succession
of various types of society. The most penetrating and
fruitful writings on this topic were those of Henri de
Saint-Simon (1760–1825). He held that the history of
civilization falls into three main periods. First there was
the period that ended with the collapse of the Roman
Empire. The prevailing religion of this first period was
polytheistic, and the social order rested upon slavery. As
a result of the barbarian invasions this social order was
succeeded by a new one in which a monotheistic religion
was associated with the feudal system. This second epoch,
Saint-Simon believed, was in process of being replaced
by a new industrial order in which monotheistic religion
was being ousted in favour of a belief in positive science.
Saint-Simon also held that the periods of transition from
one civilization to another were periods of intellectual
criticism and political upheaval. One such period of
criticism and breakdown was that which followed the fall
of the Roman Empire. Another such period was that in
which Saint-Simon and his contemporaries were living, a
time when the feudal system was in its last throes and
industrialism was being born. The feudal-theological
system harboured within itself "the germ of its own
destruction", for although it was fundamentally agricultural and military, it fostered the growth of the natural
sciences and allowed the establishment of trading classes
in the cities who possessed property of a non-feudal type.
This idea that a type of civilization may contain within
itself elements that will eventually destroy it and be the

basis of a new civilization, greatly influenced Marx and Engels. Another feature of Saint-Simon's view that also entered into Marxism was the assertion that specific types of social organization (e.g. feudalism) were closely associated with specific types of outlook or belief (e.g. monotheism). Directly connected with this is the suggestion that in periods of transition from one civilization to another there is both a clash of ideas (e.g. those who uphold the scientific outlook attack supporters of the medieval religious beliefs) and a clash of classes (e.g. the new industrial classes oppose the interests of the feudal landlords).

Thus Saint-Simon had endeavoured to distinguish the main epochs of history, to show how they differed from one another in their main social structure, and to indicate how the transition from one to another takes place. Auguste Comte, who had been Saint-Simon's secretary, elaborated a somewhat similar system, according to which mankind passes from a theological stage of development in which he understands the world in terms of gods or spirits, a metaphysical stage in which he thinks in terms of unexperienced principles or forces, and a positive stage in which his views and organizations are based on experience and experimental science. Like Saint-Simon, Comte held that both the ideas and the social characteristics of the new society came to birth inside the old society, and like Saint-Simon too, he hoped that the transition would be gradual and peaceful.

During this period when French revolutionaries and social critics were thinking in terms of dying epochs and of a new era, philosophers too were endeavouring to descry the course and destination of human history. The idealist philosophers, we have already mentioned, all concerned themselves with this topic. We have seen that a central feature of idealist philosophy was the concept of human freedom, for idealists rejected materialism and empiricism because they thought that these outlooks were incompatible with the possibility of free and rational choice. Kant's discussion of the philosophy of history was undogmatic and tentative, but he did suggest that the apparent injustices and failures of history might be necessary steps leading towards a free and peaceful social order. It was not unreasonable to hope, Kant believed, that the vicissitudes of human history would emerge into a period of freedom and perpetual peace. Fichte gave a great deal of attention to the problem of historical epochs, and argued that each epoch must correspond with a phase of rational development. In early, traditional societies, he held, reason is present but operates automatically and unselfconsciously. The men living in such an era see human society as something that works according to laws of its own, to which men have not contributed and to which they must conform. To men in this condition history appears as something foreign to them in whose processes they are caught up and lost. When they come to think consciously about themselves and their purposes, they regard reason as an authority that prescribes conduct for them. At a further stage they revolt against this authority, and indeed against all authority, as they have come to regard reason as something which they themselves prescribe, as the exercise of their own freedom. According to Fichte, therefore, human history is moving towards a stage in which it is freely created by men who not only understand but have the art of rational behaviour. In the culminating age of mankind, according to Fichte, men's knowledge and their free activity will be in unison, and history will be under their free and rational control.

This idea that men might sometime create their own history in unfettered, rational freedom, captivated Marx and Engels. But, as we have seen, the philosophical system which chiefly influenced them was that of Hegel. Like the other idealist philosophers Hegel believed that the course of human history was a development towards greater freedom. Peoples who have as yet failed to organize themselves into states, he thought, can hardly be regarded as participating in history, and so he omitted from his account of history those African and Australian tribes which lived without state government. In the oriental states of antiquity such as Egypt and Persia, one man ruled despotically, and one man only was free, the despot himself. In the Greek world, where small groups controlled the state, a few men were free. In the Germanic or Christian world, although there was still a great deal of oppression, the Reformation had adumbrated the freedom of all men with its doctrine of the priesthood of all true believers, and the French Revolution had made this doctrine of universal freedom a political reality. Hegel believed that at each stage of history one particular nation achieves the fullness of what is possible at the time and then exhausts itself when its task is completed, only to be succeeded by another nation which develops another theme in the great symphony of history. Furthermore, the rise and fall of the world-historical nations takes place through conflict and war. Thus freedom develops through struggle and defeat, and human history is a sort of harsh debate, a bloody dialectic.

This last word brings us to an important feature of Hegel's philosophy which we have mentioned but have not yet discussed. Hegel believed that the correct philosophical method was to state a thesis, to show that there are contradictions latent in it, and to overcome the contradictions by eliciting a synthesis which unites them. This is called the dialectical method, and it is one of the methods, although not the only one, that philosophers have utilized since Socrates used the method of dialogue in ancient Athens. Hegel, like Fichte before him, placed this method at the centre of his philosophy. It was not inappropriate for him to do so, since as an idealist he believed that what is ultimately real is mind or spirit, and if this is so then there is some plausibility in the idea that everything, even the material and animal world, must partake of the nature of dialogue, the life of mind, even if the dialogue is in some cases subdued or disguised. In his *Philosophy of Right* (a work which Marx as a young man had commented upon in some detail) and in his *Lectures on the Philosophy of History*, Hegel had endeavoured to show that the progress towards freedom takes place through dialectical oscillations and that nothing good is achieved without opposition and struggle. Marx, we have seen, rejected Hegel's idealism, but he did not reject Hegel's dialectical view of history. Hegel, on the other hand, made no attempt to predict future forms of civilization, whereas Marx, as we shall see, was confident that he could do this. In this respect, he followed Condorcet, who believed that the historical past provides evidence that makes possible the scientific prediction of the human future, and Saint-Simon, who had maintained that the future society is somehow implicit in the present.

We have now had a view of some of the problems about history which were being discussed at the time when Marx and Engels began to collaborate. The continuous growth of experimental science suggested the possibility of continuous intellectual and moral progress. Geologists were dividing the history of the earth into epochs, and archaeologists were dividing the prehistory of mankind into Ages determined by the nature of the tools they had discovered. The impact of industrialism had led Saint-Simon and Comte to ask how the scientific-industrial society then emerging had been able to come to birth from the theologico-feudal society that had hitherto existed. The idealist philosophers had used the concepts of freedom and reason as clues to the course of history and had said that the culmination of history must be a society that is consciously created and controlled. All of these speculations played their part in generating the theory of historical materialism.

§2 *Historical Materialism in Outline*

We have seen that Marx used the term "materialism" for a this-worldly view from which everything supernatural had been excluded. A materialist account of things, according to Marx, is an account in terms of natural events or natural processes that can be experienced through the sense organs. A materialist account or explanation of historical events, therefore, would describe or explain them in terms of natural phenomena. But there are many such phenomena that might possibly be used in explaining the course of history, as far as it can be explained at all. Climate, soil and the prevalent type of plant and animal life might have a preponderant influence upon history, as many have thought they do. Those who are impressed by such facts have formulated a Geographical Theory of History. The biological struggle for existence or the rather more sophisticated struggle for domination have been thought by some to justify a Biological Theory of History. Others have taught that civilization is based on the fundamental instinct of sex and is at the same time a repression and a refinement of it. We might call this a Sexual Theory of History. Geographical, biological or sexual theories of history might all, therefore, be called types of historical materialism, but they are not the historical materialism of Marx and Engels. Let us consider, then, the brief statement of their view given by them in *The Communist Manifesto:*

Does it require deep insight to grasp that men's ideas, outlooks and concepts, in a word, their consciousness, changes with the conditions of their life, with their social relationships and with their social existence?

What else does the history of ideas prove than that intellectual production alters as material production alters? The ruling ideas of a time always were the ideas of the ruling class.

People speak of ideas which revolutionize a whole society; in so speaking they are only expressing the fact that within the old society the elements of a new society have formed, that the dissolution of the old ideas keeps step with the dissolution of the old conditions of life.

The authors go on to illustrate this by reference to the rise of bourgeois-capitalist society. In the eighteenth century, particularly in France, there was a movement, now known as the Enlightenment, which was highly critical of traditional philosophical, political and religious beliefs. Marx and Engels believed that thinkers of the Enlightenment destroyed the effectiveness of the Christian religion at the very time when the bourgeois revolutionaries were destroying the feudal regime by the Revolution of 1789. They also held that the liberal belief in freedom of religion and freedom of conscience was nothing but an expression in the sphere of knowledge of that free competition in economic affairs which the new capitalists were demanding.

It is clear that in this passage of *The Communist Manifesto* Marx and Engels are concerned with revolutions and with the part played in them by ideas and ideals. Their view is that there is something basic in human society, which they call "conditions of life", "social relationships" and "social existence". It is in this basic aspect of society that changes first take place, and changes in "ideas, outlooks and concepts" follow after. This, of course, contradicts the beliefs of most of those taking part in social movements and political revolutions, who believe that they are altering society by putting forward new ideas, new outlooks and new concepts. Thus Marx and Engels are saying that it is not ideas that change history but changes in men's "conditions of life" which change ideas and history with them. In this passage little is said about the basic aspect of society, the "conditions of life", but the one thing that is said is important, for the expression "material production" is used.

Included in the "conditions of life", then, is material production, and as this alters, intellectual (or spiritual) production alters too. Basic in society, then, is production of material things presumably by material means, and the contention is that the production of ideas, outlooks and concepts alters with, and as a result of changes in, material production. Material production means such activities as growing and harvesting crops, and making tools and clothes. Hence the view being advanced by Marx and Engels is that changes in men's ideas, outlooks and concepts follow changes in the methods of producing material goods. The moving force in society is material production, while intellectual or spiritual production is somehow secondary.

We may note also that Saint-Simon's theory of the way in which civilizations are transformed is incorporated into the theory of revolution expounded in *The Communist Manifesto*. For Marx and Engels say that when radical intellectual attacks are being made upon a form of society, this means that the elements of a new form of society have been engendered within it and are creating a new outlook and new concepts as the old form of society begins to decline. They also refer to classes, and in so doing they borrow another element of Saint-Simon's theory, for, like Marx and Engels, Saint-Simon had believed that the traders and industrialists of capitalist society had evolved from the traders who had been allowed by the nobility to live and work on sufferance in the towns of feudal society. The theme of class conflict is central to *The Communist Manifesto*, but whereas Saint-Simon, who had fought for the colonists in the American Revolution and had been in danger of his life in the

French Revolution, hoped that the new order could come without bloodshed, Marx and Engels were not averse to the possibility of violence. In *The Communist Manifesto*, again, Marx and Engels look forward to the victory of the proletariat over the bourgeoisie, whereas Saint-Simon considered that employers and workmen together formed a single interest in society which would break the power of the non-productive, lazy classes. On this matter Saint-Simon seems to have made the more fortunate guess, for in twentieth-century capitalism trades' unions and managements generally band together at the expense of consumers and shareholders.

Marx went to London in 1849 and lived there for the rest of his life, subsisting, somewhat precariously, on constant subventions from Engels and on what he could get from articles he contributed to newspapers. He took with him from Paris an unfinished book which he had worked on in 1844 after the beginning of his association with Engels. This was not published until long after Marx and Engels were dead, and we can now see in it the first draft of a comprehensive treatise on economics and society which Marx was trying all his life to bring to completion. This first draft is generally referred to as the *Economic and Philosophical Manuscripts of 1844*. It shows the great influence on Marx of Hegel and of Feuerbach, and it shows, too, that Marx had come to believe that in capitalist society the individual worker was forced to sell himself in selling his labour. As Engels had already done in his *Sketch of a Critique of Political Economy*, Marx endeavoured to show that in capitalist society the individuals by their unplanned activities produced a social network in which they were trapped, much as they

regarded themselves as subjects and worshippers of a
Supreme Being when in fact He was really their own
creation. In a socialist or communist society they would
be free from this "alienation" and this "self-estrange-
ment", to use two words which Marx borrowed from
Hegel and Feuerbach. In this unfinished work there is
also an attack on the way in which money, in a capitalist
society, is able to buy services and to corrupt the most
valuable human relationships. Here the influence of
Carlyle's attack on "the cash nexus" is apparent. "Cash
Payment", Carlyle had written in *Chartism* (1839) "has
become the sole nexus of man to man." "Money," wrote
Marx in these manuscripts, "is the pimp between need and
the object, between human life and the means of life".

Once he was established in London, Marx set to work
in an attempt to complete this treatise. He did an
enormous amount of research in the Reading Room of the
British Museum and by 1857–8 he had produced a rough
draft of very considerable length. He neither completed
nor published this (it was first published in Moscow in
1939 and 1941), and in 1859 there appeared instead in
Berlin in German a shorter book entitled *Towards a
Critique of Political Economy*, Volume I. The second
volume was never written. It is the Preface to this
Critique of Political Economy that concerns us here,
because it contains the most adequate statement of the
theory of Historical Materialism that Marx ever published. Marx here refers to Engels' *Outlines of a Critique
of Political Economy* of 1844 and to the unpublished book
they had collaborated in, *The German Ideology* of 1846.
He also refers, however, to his own article on Hegel's
Philosophy of Right, published in 1844, and to the

considerations it gave rise to. It is clear, therefore, that Marx himself believed that the theory of Historical Materialism arose out of his earlier reflections on religion and law. This is what Marx wrote in 1859 in the Preface to *Towards a Critique of Political Economy:*

The first work, undertaken to settle the doubts that assailed me, was a critical revision of Hegel's Philosophy of Right, a work, the introduction to which appeared in Paris in 1844 in the *Deutsch-Französische Jahrbücher.* My investigation led to the result that legal relations and forms of state cannot be understood from themselves nor from the so-called general development of the human mind, but have their roots rather in the material conditions of life, the aggregate of which Hegel, following the procedure of the English and French of the eighteenth century, grouped under the name of "civil society", but that the anatomy of civil society is to be found in political economy. I began to study the latter in Paris and continued it in Brussels where I had settled in consequence of an expulsion-order issued by M. Guizot. The general result that emerged and which, once reached, served as the guiding thread in my studies, can be briefly formulated as follows: In the social production of their subsistence, men enter into definite, necessary relationships that are independent of their will, relationships of production which correspond to a definite stage of development of their material forces of production. The aggregate of these relationships of production forms the economic structure of society, the real basis on which a juridical and political superstructure arises, and to which definite social forms of consciousness correspond. The mode of production of the material means of subsistence determines the social, political and spiritual life-process as a whole. It is not the consciousness of men that determines their being, but on the contrary it is their social being that determines their consciousness. At a certain stage of their development the material forces of production of the society come into contradiction with the existing relationships of production, or, what is only a legal expression for these, with the property-relationships within which they had hitherto moved. From being forms of development of the forces of production these relationships are transformed into their fetters. There then comes a period of social revolution. With the change in the economic production the whole huge superstructure is slowly or rapidly revolutionized. In considering such revolutions one should always distinguish between the material revolution in the economic conditions of production which can be faithfully substantiated by the methods of the natural sciences, and the juridical, political, religious, artistic, in brief, the ideological forms in which men become conscious of this conflict and fight it out. Just as we do not judge what an individual is from what he thinks about himself, so we cannot judge an epoch of revolution from its own consciousness, but on the contrary we must explain this consciousness from the contradictions of material life, from the existing conflict between social forces of production and relationships of production. A social system never perishes before all the forces of production have developed for which it is sufficiently large, and new, higher relationships of production never come into being before the material conditions for their existence have been incubated in the womb of the old society itself. Therefore, mankind only sets itself problems which it can solve, for when we look closely we shall always find that the problem itself only arises where the material conditions for its solution are already in existence or at least just in process of becoming. In broad outline, the Asiatic, ancient, feudal and modern bourgeois modes of production can be described as progressive epochs of the economic structure of society. The bourgeois relationships of production are the last antagonistic form of the social process of production, antagonistic, not in the sense of individual antagonism, but in the sense of an antagonism that grows out of the social conditions of the life of the individuals. But the forces of production developing in the womb of bourgeois society create at the same time the material conditions for the resolution of this antagonism and with this social system, therefore, the pre-history of human society is brought to a close.

The view set out in this passage is an elaboration of the passage we quoted from *The Communist Manifesto*. There is the same distinction between what is basic in society and ideas, outlooks and concepts, which in *Towards a Critique of Political Economy* are called "ideological forms". In *The Communist Manifesto* the basic aspect is described as "conditions of life" and there is reference to production. In *Towards a Critique of Political Economy* the basic aspect is described as "civil society" and this in its turn is said to have "political economy" as its "anatomy". A further reference to "economic conditions of production" confirms the importance of economic factors in the basis of society. The Saint-Simonian account of social change and of revolution is repeated, but it is now said that the antagonisms of bourgeois society will be ended and that this will also be the end of "the pre-history of human society". The implication is that history itself will only begin when the revolution against capitalism has ended in victory. We must now attempt to give an analysis and explanation of these assertions.

§3 *Basis and Superstructure*

Marx's first assertion is that legal relations and forms of state are not self-explanatory but need to be understood in terms of "the material conditions of life" or of what English and French writers of the eighteenth century had called "civil society". The English (or rather Scottish) writer Marx had in mind is Adam Ferguson who, in his *Essay on the History of Civil Society* (1766), had argued that the improvement of the "commercial arts" can be taken as an indication of the development of civilization. Furthermore, Ferguson had endeavoured to base his history of "civil society" upon the means used at various periods in order to obtain a living. At the savage level, for example, men gathered food and went hunting; at the level of barbarism they had learnt to make pots, to tame domestic animals, to grow crops and to work metals; at the level of civilization they discovered the art of writing. Ferguson's *History of Civil Society* was not concerned with the rise and fall of heroes, kings and dynasties, but with social transformations of a more pervasive and fundamental kind, and this is part of what Marx meant by "civil society". Saint-Simon had read Ferguson and had incorporated some of these ideas in his view that industrial society is of more importance than that part of society that promotes and engages in politics and wars. Still a further source of this notion was Hegel, who in his *Philosophy of Right* used the expression "civil society" for that aspect of society in which individuals seek their own interests by competitive production and commerce. Thus when Marx says that legal relations and forms of state have their roots in civil society, he means that they have their roots in what we might call the business side

of life, in modes of production, types of product, methods
of exchange and distribution.

The "material conditions of life", or "civil society" are
distinguished by Marx into two aspects, the "forces of
production" and the "relations of production". By the
former he appears to mean the types of technique and
of tools and machines which men use to preserve and to
further their life-activities. Among "forces of production"
there would be included agriculture, hunting, the use of
windmills, steam power, and so on. It is not quite so
clear what he means by "relations of production", but
they must be forms of organization that go beyond
industry or business in its narrowest sense, since he says
not only that relations of production can correspond with
a stage of development of the material forces of production, but also that they can conflict with the forces of
production. Relations of production, therefore, must be
such things as types of property, property in men, for
example, or in land, chattels or company shares, or the
ways in which goods are distributed and used. Unfortunately Marx is very sparing of examples to illustrate
this view, but in *The Communist Manifesto* he had said
that as capitalist industrial production developed it
became incompatible with retention of the existing
feudal organization, and in particular with "the feudal
relations of property". These became fetters constraining
the growth of the developing system. "They had to be
burst asunder; they were burst asunder." Feudal methods
of farming involving strips and common land, prohibitions
on the movement of men and of commodities, tithes and
tariffs, were relations of production associated with
dying forces of production. If these feudal relations of

production had been persisted in, they would have prevented the growth of new forms of agricultural and industrial production which, as forms of production, were superior to the old. Their technical superiority must in the end lead to their prevalence. Superior productive forces must finally establish relations of production that enable them to operate effectively.

In our examination of Marx's theory of history, we have not yet reached beyond or above the basis. But the basis itself is obviously not all of a piece, for within it Marx distinguished between the forces of production and the relations of production. It is the forces of production which, in his view, are *ultimately* basic, since although the relations of production can pull against them for a time they must finally be brought into line with them. Under the heading "forces of production" Marx must have included such things as food-gathering at one stage of social development, agriculture at another stage, and the use of steam power at yet another stage. His idea is that when a more effective productive force has been invented, say agriculture, then it will drive out the earlier, less effective forces and the types of property that went with them. In a society of food-gatherers private property would hardly be necessary, so agriculture could not drive that out, but, once established, agriculture would make food-gathering over-laborious and even pointless. Furthermore, if agriculture is to proceed, people must be kept from trampling down the growing crops by walking over them, and hence property in land, hitherto non-existent, becomes a necessity. Hostility on the part of food-gatherers to rules against trampling the crops would at the same time be hostility to agriculture and to the benefits it brings. So the fetters, in this case hostility to the enclosure of land, must be burst asunder, and burst asunder they are.

But must they be? Agricultural production is so very much superior to grubbing around in pursuit of roots and berries that it is not surprising that it got established along with the sorts of land enclosure that were necessary for it. But the superior technique or instrument is not always adopted, at least not straight away. In the twenties and thirties of the nineteenth century, for example, a new type of steam-carriage was introduced on to the roads, in London and elsewhere. These provided faster and better transport than what was obtainable from the use of horse-drawn carriages. But the coaching interests, alarmed at the possibility of losing their livelihood, brought their influence to bear upon Parliament so that absurdly low limits were placed upon the speeds at which the steam-carriages were allowed to go. This drove them off the roads, and when steam traction was reintroduced a little later, it was along privately owned tracks. But if the original steam-carriages had not been prevented from operating, it might not have been necessary for railways to be constructed as in fact they were. If goods and people had been carried by road in the eighteen-thirties, there might have been no Railway Age. Population might have settled in different places, there might have been more but smaller towns, and the face of the country might have been very different indeed.

To this it may be objected that although the coaching interests, which were a part of the old relations of production, succeeded in retarding steam locomotion for a while, and thus succeeded in holding back a new form of production, they were only able to do this for a short time. This is so, but in consequence of this delaying action the new industrial age took a very different form from what it would have done without it. In this case, and no doubt in many others, the relations of production which, according to Marx, belonged to an outmoded set of productive forces, modified the operation of the new productive forces in very important ways. The steam locomotives did not run on the public highways, and the railway companies had to buy land for private tracks. In doing this they submitted themselves not only to an Act of Parliament but also to the existing laws about property, even though they had to get parliamentary approval of what they proposed to do. There is no such sharp break between one epoch and another as Marx said there was. In Germany, as Marx knew, the freedom of trade that was widely regarded as necessary for capitalist advance was never granted, so that controls over commerce persisted from the pre-capitalist into the capitalist era. In our own day, indeed, all sorts of mercantilist devices such as tariffs, state monopolies and export subsidies have persisted or have been revived in capitalist societies. Nor should it be overlooked that in Great Britain intelligent feudal aristocrats engaged in capitalist enterprises of their own and found means of reconciling what, on grounds of Marxist theory, should have been mutually contradictory activities. Something was done which, if Marx was right, could not possibly have been done.

It appears, then, that Marx's revolutionary zeal led him to over-emphasize the breaks between one historical period and another and to underestimate the continuities between them. But we must now ask whether Marx really expressed his theory coherently, whether the main concepts he used in it are consistent or adequately defined. The fundamental concepts are, first, the concept of a basis. This basis is distinguished into two parts or aspects, the forces of production on the one hand and the relations of production on the other. The forces of production, we have seen, are, if the expression may be allowed, more ultimate than the relations of production, and the latter have their "legal expression" in property-relationships. Marx uses the term "civil society" for this whole complex basis and says that its anatomy is found in political economy. Then he distinguishes between the basis of society and its superstructure. In the Preface of *Towards a Critique of Political Economy*, Marx mentions the legal and political superstructure and the "ideological forms".

Now if property-relationships are the legal expression of the relations of production, then it would seem that at any rate the law of property belongs to the basis. Yet on the other hand, Marx writes as if law belongs to the superstructure along with politics. This is just one of many problems of interpretation which this important passage gives rise to. Another fundamental problem of interpretation is this: did Marx intend to assert that the ultimate source of social and historical change is to be found in the forces of production alone? Did he hold, that is, that no important social or historical change takes place except as a consequence of changes in the forces of production? If he did hold this, then he was really putting forward a technological theory of history. If he held, on the other hand, that it is changes in the basis as a whole, in productive relations as well as productive forces, that bring about all other important social and historical changes, then his theory would be better described as an economico-technological theory of history. Can we say which it was of the these theories that Marx really held? Unfortunately we can not, since Marx himself was far from clear on the matter. But we must look elsewhere in his writings for more evidence about what he really meant.

§4 *The Technological Theory of History*

That Marx himself was not altogether clear about the exact nature of his own theory may be seen if we briefly compare the terminology he used in two letters he wrote to Engels. In the first of these, written on 25th September 1857, Marx says that the theory held by Engels and himself asserts "the connection of the productive forces and social relations". In the second, written on 7th July, 1866, a year before the publication of Volume I of *Capital*, Marx wrote of "the determination of the organization of labour by the means of production". In the one letter it will be seen, Marx said that the productive forces are *connected with* social relations, and in the other that they *determine* the organization of labour. Even if we ignore the difference between "connected with" and "determine", and take it that Marx really meant the latter (for how could anyone deny anything as vague as the former?), there is a very considerable difference between the organization of labour and social relations. Marx is quite right in saying that means of production determine the organization of labour. A solitary man can use a spade or hoe, for example, whereas it takes several men to handle a trawler. Different types of tool or machine determine different types of job-relationships.

Some tools can be used by one man or woman. Some machines require a whole crew or team to be in attendance. But when Marx says that productive forces are connected with social relations, it is far from clear what he means. It might mean that means of production (tools or machines) determine social relations, but we must then ask: which social relations and how? The implication would seem to be that all social relations, not merely job-relationships, are determined by the tools and machines men use. I do not doubt that Marx meant something of the sort. It would certainly constitute a technological theory of society and of history, and we must now ask whether Marx expressed such a theory in his more considered writings.

The most celebrated passage in Marx's writings in which he appears to express a technological theory of history occurs in *The Poverty of Philosophy*, the book attacking Proudhon which appeared in 1847. Here Marx writes:

M. Proudhon the economist understands well enough that men make cloth, linen or silk materials in definite relations of production. But what he has not understood is that these definite social relations are just as much produced by men as linen, flax, etc. Social relations are closely bound up with productive forces. In acquiring new productive forces men change their mode of production, and in changing their mode of production, their way of earning their living, they change all their social relations. The hand-mill gives you society with the feudal lord, the steam-mill, society with the industrial capitalist.

But the same men who establish their social relations in conformity with their material productivity, produce also

principles, ideas and categories, in conformity with their social relationships.

Thus these ideas, these categories are as little eternal as the relations they express. They are *historical and transitory products*.

We live in the midst of a continual movement of growth in the productive forces, of destruction in social relations, of formation in ideas; the only immutable thing is the abstraction of movement—*mors immortalis*.

The doctrine here set forth is concentrated in the statement that the hand-mill gives you society with the feudal lord, the steam-mill society with the industrial capitalist. The idea is that hand-mills bring about feudal society and steam-mills bring about industrial capitalism. Of course we need not take this literally. Marx probably means that hand-mills *and such like means of production* bring about feudal society, and that steam-mills *and other sorts of power-driven machinery* bring about capitalist society. This is an assertion of the technological theory of history, and it is important for us to examine closely how Marx supports it.

In this passage, then, Marx begins by saying that when men make cloth, etc., they do so in definite relations of production. By this Marx appears to mean that in order to make cloth, etc., the makers have to be organized in factories or workshops in the way that the tools and machines they use require them to be. If this is the point he is making, then by "definite relations of production" he means what in his letter of 7th July, 1866, he called the "organization of labour". Marx then goes on to say that these relations of production are *produced* by men just as the cloth is produced by them. This is a step in his

exposition that is missing from the passage we have considered in the *Critique of Political Economy*. It is important because it serves to bridge the gap between forces of production and relations of production with the assertion that the latter are produced by the former. Thus Marx says that when men use tools and machines they produce not only goods or commodities but also the job-relationships in which they are organized. But he then passes on from job-relationships to "social relations" which he says are "closely bound up with productive forces". How does this come about? According to Marx, new methods of production bring new job-relationships, and these in their turn bring new ways in which men earn their living.

Marx, here as elsewhere, gives no examples, so we must try to illustrate his point in our own way. When steam locomotion was introduced, coach-drivers were replaced by engine-drivers and a new class of workers, plate-layers, came into existence. Engine-drivers might be rather like coach-drivers in their working lives, but there had never been any plate-layers before, and to that extent a new mode of livelihood was created by the new productive force. And so Marx says: "they change their way of earning their living—they change all their social relations". But *do* they change all their social relations? Of course, engine-drivers and plate-layers have different sorts of *working lives* from those of coach-drivers and road-menders. But it does not follow that their *social relationships outside their working lives* are so very different from those of their coaching and road-mending predecessors. Engine-drivers and plate-layers occupy rather humble positions in society, much as coachmen and road-menders had done. It may be said, however, that a coach-driver in the coaching age could own and drive his own coach, whereas no engine-driver ever owned his own locomotive. Returning to our example of the steam-carriages, however, we may remark that, but for the opposition of the coaching interests, individuals might possibly have owned and driven their own steam-carriages. It was partly because of legislation against the steam-carriages that railway companies bought land on which to run their locomotives. The new relations of production, then, as distinct from mere job-relationships, took the form they did as a result of interplay between old and new and not solely because of the nature of the new productive forces. When new technological inventions are adopted, the social conditions within which they operate are not determined solely by the nature of the invention itself, but also by give and take with the social conditions that already exist.

§5 *Man as a Tool-making Animal*

So far we have examined various passages in which Marx expounded his theory of historical materialism. In none of those considered so far, however, does he give any reasons in favour of the view. One might expect that a view of this scope and importance would be supported by references to a great number of historical events, but Marx does not do this, so perhaps he intended his theory to be the sort that is based on some fundamental analysis of human nature and human life. In the passage from *The Communist Manifesto* we have already considered, Marx and Engels begin by asking whether it requires deep insight to grasp that men's consciousness changes with the conditions of their life. Clearly they did not think it did require deep insight. Of course, *The Communist Manifesto* was not mainly drafted as a piece of scientific and philosophical argumentation, but even if we recognize this and look elsewhere for Marx's reasons, we do not find it easy to disengage them from what seem to be mere assertions. Near the beginning of *The German Ideology*, however, Marx and Engels give what seems to me to be the chief reason in favour of their theory. The passage runs as follows:

> Men can be distinguished from animals by consciousness, by religion or anything else you like. They themselves begin to distinguish themselves from animals as soon as they begin to *produce* their means of subsistence, a step which is conditioned by their bodily organization. By producing their means of subsistence men are indirectly producing their material life itself.
>
> The way in which men produce their means of subsistence depends first of all on the nature of the means of subsistence they find in being and have to reproduce. This mode of production must not be considered simply as being the reproduction of the physical existence of the individuals. Rather it is a definite form of the activity of these individuals, a definite form of expressing their life, a definite *mode of life* on their part. As individuals express their life, so they are. What they are, therefore, coincides with their production, both with *what* they produce and with *how* they produce. What individuals are thus depends on the material conditions determining their production.

The first thing that Marx and Engels say in this important passage is that there are various *arbitrary* ways in which men may be distinguished from animals, but that the way of distinguishing them from animals that is inherent in men themselves is the fact that they produce their means of subsistence. That is, they produce their food, their dwelling-places, their clothes, their tools. In doing this, in producing these things, they indirectly produce their material life itself. Why should it follow from their producing their means of subsistence that they also produce "their material life itself"? In the German text the nature of the transition is more clearly apparent than in the English translation. The expression "means of subsistence" is a correct translation of the German word "Lebensmittel", but a literal translation would be "means of life". Thus in German the transition from "means of subsistence" to "material life itself" is mediated by the appearance of the word for "life" in both expressions, whereas in English there is no *obvious* connection between food, dwelling-places, clothes and tools on the one hand, and "material life itself" on the other, for clothes and tools are not alive.

However, Marx and Engels support their argumentative transition from the production of means of subsistence to production of material life by reasons other than verbal ones. They say that each new human individual who comes into existence finds a stock of "means of subsistence" already in being and has to play his part in replenishing this stock. In doing this he is not only taking steps to maintain his existence as a bodily, physical being, but is also maintaining himself in a definite *way of life*. He is expressing his life in the activities he undertakes in using and replacing the means of production, in using and replacing both the tools concerned with *how* he produces and the other objects (clothes, food?) which he produces, which comprise *what* he produces. What men are, or, as one translator has it, their *nature*, is determined by the material conditions which make them the sort of men they are. If they are hunters they will live one sort of life and be one sort of men, if they are agriculturalists they will live a different sort of life and be a different sort of men.

Now two very different lines of thought are fused together in this argument. In the first place, what Marx and Engels say is influenced by Hegel's discussion of labour in his *Phenomenology of Mind* (1807). Although Hegel was an idealist, he did not think that the mind is something withdrawn and hidden from the material world. On the contrary, he believed that mind had to reveal itself in its products and that the process of work or labour was one way in which mind developed. In shaping or forming objects in the material world the worker has to overcome obstacles, resistances to his desires, but when he has made what he set out to make, his initial wish or desire has turned into the form of what he has made, and the independent product now existing outside him is at the same time his mind, is himself. He is in what he makes or creates. In a sense, therefore, the objects that men make are themselves, are, we may put it, forms of their consciousness, forms of their life. When, therefore, Marx and Engels say that men's means of subsistence "express their life", they are undoubtedly following out this Hegelian conception. But they fused it with something less metaphysical and more mundane, with the obvious fact that men's work is organized in accordance with the nature of the requisite tools and methods. The forces of work and forms of life are therefore bound together and both tools and products, the *how* and the *what* of production, express the lives of men. To understand the workings of society, therefore, it is necessary to explore its "material life", that is, its production and its products. These are the basic expressions of social life. The sequence of ideas is roughly of this order: life—work—production and products—the social order which does the producing and uses the products.

This theory received its final form in Marx's *Capital: Critique of Political Economy*, Volume I, (1867). In Chapter V, §1, entitled "The Labour Process" there appears the following passage:

We are not here concerned with the first animal and instinctive forms of labour. A great period of time has elapsed between the time when human labour had not yet got rid of its first instinctive form and the time when man entered the commodity market as the seller of his own labour-power. We are considering labour in a form in which it belongs exclusively to man. A spider carries on operations like those of a weaver, and a bee puts to shame many a human builder by the way in which it constructs its cell. But what from the very first distinguishes the worst builder from the best bee, is that the builder has built the cell in his head before he builds it in wax. At the end of the labour process a result emerges that was already in the imagination of the worker, that was already in existence in an ideal form. It is not merely that the worker brings about a change in the natural world; at the same time he realizes his purpose in the natural world; and his purpose determines the kind and manner of his action as a law governing it and as something to which he must subordinate his will.

A little further on in the same chapter Marx writes:

As soon as the labour process has developed to some degree, it has need of already fabricated instruments of labour. In the most ancient caves inhabited by men we find tools and weapons of stone. Alongside worked up stone, wood, bones and shells, animals, tamed and bred and thus altered through labour, played a principal part as instruments of labour at the beginning of human history. The use and creation of instruments of labour, although in embryo it is characteristic of certain animal species, characterizes the specifically human labour process and Franklin therefore defines man as "a tool-making animal". The remains of instruments of labour have the same importance for the study of extinct economic social formations as the structure of fossil bones has for a knowledge of extinct animal species. It is not what is made, but how, with what instruments of labour it is made that distinguishes economic epochs. Instruments of labour are not only the standard for judging the development of human labour power, but also indications of the social relationships within which the labour takes place.

If we compare these passages from *Capital* with the passage we have quoted from *The German Ideology* we notice one rather important difference. In *The German Ideology* Marx and Engels say that individuals express their lives in their production, both in *what* they produce as well as in *how* they produce it. In *Capital* Marx says that what distinguishes economic epochs is not *what* is made, but *how* it is made. Now it is surely more plausible to maintain that the nature of human society expresses human production as a whole, both the manner of producing goods and the goods themselves, than to maintain that it is the means of production only, the tools, that constitute what is essential in human activity. In *Capital* Marx seems to have moved from what we might call a material theory of history, according to which all aspects of material production are basic, to a technological theory of history, according to which it is tools and machines that are basic. According to the earlier, material theory, human society can and should be understood in terms of the means of producing goods and of the goods produced and consumed. According to the later, technological theory, human society can and should be understood in terms of the *means* of production only. In placing so much importance on Franklin's definition of man as a tool-making animal, Marx is deliberately belittling the things the tools are used to make and the use that these final products are put to. He is placing all his stress on the means of production and none on the objects consumed. This is partly because, unlike *The German Ideology, Capital* is concerned with economic theory, and Marx, like many other economists of his time, accepted the labour theory of value, according to which it was the labour put into them that bestowed economic value on things.

If we look closely at what Marx says we might conclude that he has not expressed his view exactly as he wished to. Both in *The German Ideology* and in *Capital* Marx notices that individuals come upon the scene and find a lot of material artifacts already in existence. These, in fact, are not only tools, but consumer goods as well. The important thing, I suggest, is not that men make tools, but rather that each new generation of men receives the organized collection of artifacts that other generations have produced and makes its own additions to them. Houses, roads, machines, books, improved soil, schools, insurance companies, are handed on by one generation to the next. Marx noticed that spiders and bees make things, and he says that they differ from man in that men first imagine or conceive the things they make. It is not impossible, however, that beavers have some prior imagination of the dams they build. Surely a more significant difference between the things that animals make and the things that human beings make is that the latter are constantly improved. I do not suppose that bees or beavers make any better cells or dams now than they made thousands of years ago, whereas men who once lived in caves now live in houses, men who once cut with flints now cut with knives, men who once drank brackish water now drink vintage wines.

Marx says that it is men's social being that determines their consciousness, that what men are depends on the material conditions determining their production. But social being, material conditions and forces of production do not spring up on their own. They are not merely brought about by men, but in many cases are devised or invented by them. I suggest that it is ability to invent and improve rather than the ability to plan and to make which differentiates men from animals and is responsible for the essential difference between animal and human societies. Marx recognized this important characteristic on the occasions when he referred to the way in which new generations find a set of material things and institutions waiting for them, but he misunderstood its significance when he thought that it could be adequately described as an ability to make tools. If man is to be characterized in some single and fundamental way, it is better to describe him as the animal that makes or creates than merely as the animal that makes tools, for he makes more than tools and makes tools in order to do so. He bequeaths a social inheritance for future generations to improve indefinitely. Animal production is uniformly monotonous, human production is cumulatively various.

§6 *The Economico-Technological Theory of History*

We have already suggested that Marx's account of Historical Materialism is open to two interpretations. The technological interpretation we have now discussed and it is the economico-technological interpretation which we must now briefly consider. It is this second way of understanding his view which Marx must have had in mind when he said that the anatomy of "civil society" or of "the material conditions of life" is to be found in political economy, and when he wrote of "the economic structure of society". No doubt this wider view established itself in Marx's mind because of his familiarity with the economic theories of the time according to which labour is the source of economic value, and production a major theme of economic science. Men must produce to live and in consequence economics is basic in life and society. If Marx had asserted that the economy plays an *important* part in human society and human history he would have been saying something that needed saying at the time at which he was writing, when the importance of economic factors had not been fully appreciated by all historians and social theorists. It is true that among others, Adam Smith and Saint-Simon had preceded Marx in this, but Marx developed the idea in new ways and gave an impetus to the study of social and economic history. But the observation that economic factors play an important part in history does not distinguish Marxism from the views of such writers as Thorold Rogers who in his *Economic Interpretation of History* (1888) wrote that "economical causes have had much to do with the events about which the philosopher of history dilates and prates chaotically" (7th edition, p. 250). Rogers did not, however, like Marx, hold that economic factors are the sole independent determining factors in history, but on the contrary allowed weight to religious and political factors too.

According to Marx, however, politics is part of the superstructure and religion is an "ideological form". In putting this forward he is saying that political and religious changes always follow after and as a result of economico-technological changes. One might expect that such a view would have to be supported by a mass of historical evidence collected from different places and periods. But although Marx brought forward a lot of evidence to *support* his case, he did not look around for examples that might have counted against it. His grounds for it appear to be mainly theoretical and to depend upon the theory that man is essentially or fundamentally a tool-making animal and that his other activities are dependent on this. Marx believed that politics, law and the ideologies (religion, art, etc.) *must* be secondary or tertiary social and historical phenomena by comparison with the economico-technological features of society. Why this, on Marx's view, must be so can only be understood by reference to his account of politics and the ideologies.

§7   *The Legal and Political Superstructure*

Marx's view in brief is that law and politics are subordinate to technology and economics. He means that no fundamental political change can be understood in political terms but must receive its explanation in terms of the economic structure of society. We don't know what is really going on until we look beyond such things as the deposition of kings and the removal of aristocratic privileges to such things as expanding markets and new methods of production. I have referred to *fundamental* political changes, because it can hardly be suggested that every political change, for example the death of a king or the success of an intrigue, must have deep economic causes. An example that was constantly in Marx's mind was the series of revolutions in France, the so-called Great Revolution of 1789 and the revolutions of 1830 and 1848.

Marx read a great deal about the Revolution of 1789 and at one time thought of writing a history of it. In *The Holy Family* there is a whole section devoted to it, and in 1852 in *The Eighteenth Brumaire of Louis Bonaparte* he prefaced his discussion of Louis Napoleon's *coup d'état* of 1851 with some comments on the significance of the earlier revolutions. Marx referred to the way in which the leaders of the Revolution of 1789 had regarded themselves as like Roman republicans establishing and maintaining the ancient republican virtues. They used the high-flown language of the ancient heroes to dignify the great historical task they obscurely felt that they were carrying out.

Camille Desmoulins, Danton, Robespierre, Saint-Just, Napoleon, the heroes as well as the parties and masses of the old French Revolution, completed in Roman dress and Roman phrases the task of their time, the releasing and the establishment of modern *bourgeois* society. The first named of these men broke the feudal basis into pieces and mowed off the feudal heads that had grown from it. The last named created within France the conditions under which free competition could be developed, the parcelled out landed property could be exploited, and the unfettered industrial productive force could be utilized. Outside the frontiers of France he everywhere swept the feudal organizations away as far as was necessary in order to provide a suitable up-to-date environment on the European continent for the bourgeois society in France. Once the new social organization was established, the antediluvian colossuses disappeared and with them the resurrected Romans—the Brutuses, Gracchuses, Publicolas, the tribunes, the senators and Caesar himself. Bourgeois society in its sober reality had produced its true interpreters and mouthpieces in the Says, Cousins, Royer-Collards, Benjamin Constants and Guizots, its real army commanders sat at financiers' desks, and the blubber-faced Louis XVIII was its political head. Completely absorbed in the production of wealth and in the peaceful battle of competition, it no longer noticed that ghosts from the days of Rome had watched over its cradle. But however unheroic bourgeois society is, it had had need of heroism, of self-sacrifice, of terror, of civil war and of battles of the nations in order to get into the world. And its gladiators found in the Roman Republic the ideals and the forms of art, the self-deceptions which they needed in order to hide from themselves the bourgeois limitations of their battles and to raise their passion to the level of the great historical tragedy. Similarly a century earlier at another level of evolution, Cromwell and the English people had borrowed speech, passions and

illusions from the Old Testament for their bourgeois
revolution. When the real aim was reached, when the
bourgeois transformation of English society was completed,
Locke supplanted Habukkuk.

There are some puzzles in this brilliant passage. For
example, Marx could not have really meant that Camille
Desmoulins, a mere journalist, and politicians such as
Danton, broke the feudal *basis* into pieces, for the basis
consists of technological and economic factors. But they
did play their part in "mowing off" the feudal heads
that had grown from the feudal basis—the king and queen
and the aristocrats who were guillotined or massacred.
What Marx does emphasize here is that these political
revolutionaries did not really understand what they were
bringing about. They looked upon themselves as Romans
attacking against tremendous odds, whereas in fact they
were making France and Europe safe for industrial
capitalism. They were "releasing and establishing
bourgeois society". That is, they were freeing it from the
feudal chains that still bound it, from legal and political
arrangements which belonged to a feudal society and
could only be trammels and hindrances to the newly
formed forces of production. They pictured themselves as
rebelling with stoic virtue against blood-stained tyrants,
whereas their republican declamations and posturings
were directed against men whose power had already been
lost. The dying pomp of feudal aristocracy was faced
and extinguished by men masquerading as Ancient
Romans whose pre-feudal civilization was even less
relevant to the economic circumstances. This heroic age
of the Revolution was followed by one in which the

bourgeois outlook was more consciously expressed, when J.-B. Say, the economist, developed the views of Adam Smith, Victor Cousin pieced together new philosophical positions, Royer-Collard combined philosophy and politics, Benjamin Constant elaborated the philosophy of liberalism and Guizot moved from historical research and interpretation to political leadership, and, as has been seen, had Marx deported from Paris. The real power was now that of the men who controlled finance and industry. The significance of "the blubber-faced Louis XVIII" was that, although the rightful heir to the throne of France as brother of the guillotined Louis XVI, he was a mere figure-head presiding over the very form of society which his brother's executioners had fought for. What, Marx is here suggesting, could more clearly show how subordinate politics and government are to the technological and economic basis of society?

In Marx's opinion the Revolution of 1830 which led to the replacement of the Bourbon Charles X by the Orléanist Louis-Philippe was a shift of influence within the bourgeois class from those closely associated with land-ownership to those among whom industrial influences predominated. Marx wrote that

The great landed property interest, in spite of its flirtation with feudalism and in spite of its pride in race, was rendered fully bourgeois through the development of modern society. Thus, the Tories in England imagined for a long time that they were enthusiasts for the monarchy, the Church and the beauties of the old English constitution, until the day of danger made them realize that they were enthusiasts only for groundrents.

As a result of the Revolution of 1848 the Orléans monarchy was overthrown and a republic established. In February 1848 a sudden outbreak of revolution removed the king and a provisional government was set up, containing various political groups, even socialists. But socialist influence was strongly resisted by the other parties and when the socialists attempted violence they were put down, as happened in the workers' risings in Paris and Lyons in June 1848. A Social-Democratic Party was formed, which set out to unite the working class with the small bourgeoisie, called by Marx the petite-bourgeoisie. Marx describes the smaller bourgeoisie as a "between-class", a class of shopkeepers and waiters.

One must not imagine that the democratic representatives are all shopkeepers or are enthusiastic for them. They can be poles apart from them in education and in personal circumstances. What makes them representatives of the smaller-bourgeoisie is that it never enters their heads to transcend the bounds which confine the lives of the smaller-bourgeoisie. Therefore these representatives are driven to the same tasks and theoretical solutions of them that the material interests and social situation of those they represent in practice force upon them. This is in general the relationship of the political and literary representatives of a class which they represent.

After giving his version of the events that followed the revolts of June, 1848, Marx says that a law of 31st May, 1850 finally brought the manoeuvring to an end and re-established the bourgeois class in supreme control.

The law of 31st May 1850 was the *coup d'état* of the bourgeoisie. All the conquests it had hitherto made against the Revolution were only provisional in character. They were put in doubt as soon as the National Assembly of the period left the scene. They now all depended upon the chances of a vote with universal suffrage, and the history of voting since 1848 conclusively proved that in the degree to which the actual rule of the bourgeoisie developed, its moral leadership over the mass of the people was lost. Universal suffrage declared itself on 10th March right against the rule of the bourgeoisie. The bourgeoisie replied with the outlawing of universal franchise. The law of 31st May was thus one of the necessities of the class struggle.

From this analysis we can see that Marx took class interests as the clue to political events. Although working men supported the revolutionaries of 1789, 1830 and 1848, it was the bourgeoisie and peasantry who gained most from them. The period 1789–93 was the heroic age of the bourgeoisie when they gained political power and used it to further the development of industry and commerce. The restored Bourbons played in, so to say, with those members of the bourgeois class who had land-owning interests. The Revolution of 1830 was the reassertion of the position of the financial and industrial wing of the bourgeois class. In this revolution, as in 1789, the working class or proletariat supported the bourgeois revolutionaries. They also supported the Revolution of 1848, but this soon became a parting of the ways. Working-class revolts were now *suppressed* by the bourgeoisie, who used the services of gangs of poor men whom Marx describes as "the ragged proletariat" (Lumpenproletariat). Small-scale bourgeoisie, shopkeepers and the like, attempted to ally themselves with the proletariat so as to mitigate the struggle between the proletariat and the bourgeoisie. Such attempts at class reconciliation, Marx believed, were doomed to failure, and he also thought them wrong as well, as in his opinion the smaller bourgeoisie are contemptible because they endeavour to withdraw from the struggle that must develop once the bourgeoisie are established as the ruling class. This struggle would be between the two opposed classes, the wage-earning, exploited proletariat and the bourgeoisie consisting of land-owning, financial and industrial capitalists and their hangers-on. In his *coup d'état* of December, 1851, Louis Napoleon had used gangs of men to assault and intimidate his opponents. Marx recognized that these men were mostly from the working classes, and he supposed that they must have been too poor and demoralized to refuse the pay they were offered. But just as the petit-bourgeois were too cowardly to affect events, so these ragged proletarians could not be of decisive influence, since they were separated from the class to which they really belonged.

We can therefore put Marx's interpretation of events in this way. There are three main factors involved in the economic production process, viz., land, labour and capital. The French Revolution of 1789 seemed to its leaders to be a rising of the people against arbitrary tyranny. Liberty, equality and fraternity were sought for all, and unjust privileges were removed. This, however, is a superficial reading of events. It is true that the peasants and workers supported the revolution against the aristocrats, but it was the bourgeoisie, the men of business and industry, who chiefly gained by it. At the Bourbon Restoration, some of the pre-revolutionary figureheads were reinstated, but in fact it was the bourgeoisie who now ruled. In 1830 the Bourbon figureheads were removed and power shifted more definitely towards the industrial capitalists. Even so, the working class supported this revolution, as they did the Revolution of 1848 in its early stages. But once it became clear that the working classes might have aims that conflicted with those of the bourgeoisie, the franchise was limited and the bourgeoisie turned against their former allies. From then onwards events had to be interpreted in terms of a struggle between two classes, the bourgeois ruling class and the proletarian exploited class. The formation of parties, the introduction of legislation, the adoption of illegal measures, were forms taken by this overmastering struggle. The distinctions within the bourgeoisie between industrialists and agriculturalists and the distinction between large and small capitalists, are relatively unimportant. What is important is that some men live by employing others to work for wages and most men live by selling their labour so that their employers may make profits. The struggle which determines the major political movements is that between profit-makers and wage-earners. The politics of capitalist society is the politics of holding the working classes in check. Whether this is done by democratic or dictatorial means depends on circumstances. The distinction between democrats and anti-democrats is secondary and evanescent, that between proletariat and capitalist is primary and decisive. That is how Marx interpreted the politics of his time.

§8 *The Ideological Superstructure*

Political movements then, according to Marx and Engels, depend upon technological and economic movements, and political groupings and manoeuvrings are surface phenomena by comparison with the conflicts of economic interest that give rise to them. But political regimes and governments and parties justify their proceedings by reference to doctrines, theories and philosophies, by what in *The Communist Manifesto*, Marx and Engels called "ideas, outlooks and concepts". The men who produce these doctrines and theories are still further removed from the industrial and economic fundamentals of social life than the kings and politicians, and hence there is an *ideological* superstructure in need of even more interpretation than the political superstructure. What men *say* about what they are doing and why they are doing it cannot be relied upon as an account of what they are really doing. This is not necessarily because they are lying, but because they do not understand the forces that are moving society, and with society themselves. According to Feuerbach, religious believers think they are serving a supernatural Creator when in reality they are celebrating the achievements of mankind or are indulging in wishful thinking. They are misled by illusions which arise from their earthly circumstances. According to Marx and Engels, this is the position of most of those men who write books on moral and political philosophy, who write plays and novels, and even of those who compose music and paint pictures. They look upon themselves as maintaining and creating the culture of their society, whereas it is trade and industry that do this while they merely justify or decorate what they do not fully comprehend. They are symptoms rather than causes, surface phenomena rather than underlying reality. Interpreting what they say in their own terms is rather like accepting what Freud later called *the manifest content* of a dream as if it were all that the dream signified. Those who grasp what is really going on in industry and trade, however, can interpret these ideological productions, much as the interpreter of dreams explains them in terms of the *latent content*. Like Feuerbach before him and Freud after him (see David Stafford-Clark, *What Freud Really Said,* Schocken Books, 1967, Chapter 3, especially pp. 63–4), Marx employed this method of seeking to elicit the basic from the derivative, to penetrate the disguise, to *dis*-illusion. Those who can practise the method of historical materialism can understand what religious apologists, philosophers and artists are doing better than they can themselves.

Marx and Engels formulated the theory of ideologies in their unpublished book, *The German Ideology*. This, as the title indicates, was concerned with the illusory philosophies and doctrines current in Germany at the time they wrote the book. They were thinking of the Hegelian philosophy and of the various philosophers such as the "Young Hegelians" who claimed to criticize and develop it. The men whom Marx and Engels were criticizing interpreted the reality of life in Germany in terms of their own ideas, but Marx and Engels claimed to interpret their ideas in terms of the German reality. This is what they wrote about the place of ideology in society:

The production of ideas, conceptions, of consciousness is at first directly interwoven with the material activity and the material commerce of men, the language of real life. Conceiving, thinking, the mental commerce of men, appears here as the direct efflux of their material behaviour.

The same is true of mental production, as it shows itself in the language of the politics, of the law, the morality, the religion, the metaphysics, etc., of a people. Men are the producers of their conceptions, ideas, etc., but real, active men, as they are conditioned by a definite development of their productive forces and of the reciprocal relationships corresponding to them up to their most extensive forms. Consciousness can never be anything else but conscious being, and the being of men is their actual life-process. If in the whole of ideology men and their circumstances appear upside down as in a *camera obscura*, this phenomenon arises from their historical life-process just as the inversion of objects on the retina arises from their directly physical life-process.

In direct contrast to German philosophy which descends from heaven to earth, here we ascend from earth to heaven. That is, the starting-point is not from what men say, what they imagine and what they conceive, nor from men as spoken about, thought about, imagined, conceived, in order to arrive at embodied men: the starting-point is with really active men, and from this real life-process the development of their ideological reflexes and echoes of this life-process are exhibited. The shadowy forms in the brain of men are necessary sublimates of their material life-process, which is empirically establishable and linked to material pre-conditions. Morality, religion, metaphysics and the rest of ideology, and the forms of consciousness corresponding to them, thus no longer retain the semblance of independence. They have no history, no development, but men, developing their material production and their material commerce with one another alter, with this their reality, their thought and the products of their thought. It is not consciousness that determines life, but life that determines consciousness. In the first way of looking at things, the starting-point is with consciousness as the living individual; in the second, with the real living individuals themselves, as they are in real life, with consciousness considered only as *their* consciousness.

It is very important to notice what Marx and Engels here class as ideologies, or as types of ideology, and what they exclude from this category. In the first of the paragraphs we have just quoted reference is made to mental production as it shows itself in "the language of politics, of the law, the morality, the religion, the metaphysics, etc. of a people". The noun "language" governs politics, the law, moralists, religion and metaphysics, so that Marx and Engels appear to be thinking of the language in which men talk about politics, law, morality, religion and metaphysics. There is a gulf, they are arguing, between what men *say* about these things and what they are really *doing* when they concern themselves with them. Men cannot cease to be embodied creatures producing their means of life in association with their fellows, but the very conditions under which they live may lead them to *talk* as if they were, at least potentially, members of a supersensible world. The ideologies, therefore, are ways of talking in which men conceal themselves from themselves and one another. They can do this in political, legal, moral, religious and metaphysical talk.

In the second of the paragraphs quoted above, Marx and Engels mention morality, religion and metaphysics "and the rest of ideology". In neither of these lists do they mention the natural sciences, and it is most important to realize why they do not. Ideological thinking is contrasted with realistic thinking. We have already seen how

Marx and Engels accepted Feuerbach's views about the illusory nature of religious thinking. They also accepted his view that speculative philosophy (which, in *The German Ideology* they call "metaphysics") is equally misleading. The thinking that is not illusory is that which is based on sense-experience of the world in which men live and work. Men's "life-processes" can be observed, described and interpreted without illusions. They are, Marx and Engels say, "empirically establishable". Marx uses a similar expression in the *Critique of Political Economy*, when, in the Preface, he says that the economic conditions of production can be "faithfully substantiated by the methods of the natural sciences". The ideas of natural scientists, therefore, are not illusory, nor are the ideas put forward by Marx and Engels when they subject human society to realistic scientific analysis. It should be noticed, too, that when Marx writes of the "ideological forms" in the *Critique of Political Economy* he does not include morality among them but does include art. We shall see later that there are obscurities in Marx's account of morality.

When Marx and Engels write of "ideologists" they are not referring to members of any specific *social class*. The division of society into social classes is a consequence of its economics and technology and the types of property connected with them. In modern society there are real divisions into landowners and capitalists on the one hand and wage-earners or proletarians on the other. On the Marxist view these class distinctions and the subdivisions within them are objective distinctions and divisions in the facts of society itself. These distinctions are *really* there, even though there are people who would like to deny them.

Furthermore, they give rise to real oppositions and conflicts in the lives of men. The pronouncements and arguments of ideologists, on the other hand, result from these real oppositions and conflicts, but do not initiate or create them. Ideologists are a sort of shadow boxers, who, by some strange misunderstanding, believe they are landing real blows in the course of real fights. They can be compared with those small boys who pretend and perhaps for a while believe that they are driving the bus when they turn an imaginary steering wheel from their seat behind the driver.

We may now see that Marx and Engels conceived themselves to have laid the foundations of an empirical science of society. In society taken as it is at a given time, the industrial and economic processes of life are the basis of everything else, of law and politics, of religion, philosophy and culture generally. The prime causes of social change are also to be found in the industrial and economic processes of life. Social change takes place through class conflict, and the conflicting classes can be objectively distinguished from one another in terms of their relation to the basic industrial and economic conditions. With this scientific knowledge of society at their disposal, historians can distinguish the main epochs of history on objective grounds. Indeed, when the notions of basis and superstructure, of class and ideology, of revolution and class-domination are properly understood, history can be transformed into a science.

§9 *Historical Dialectics*

We have already mentioned Hegel's account of human

history as a dialectic in which freedom emerges in different forms as nations struggle with one another, achieve their missions and are overcome by other nations with new missions to perform. This was the background which must have affected the conception of human history that Marx and Engels came to adopt, and it is natural to suppose that their theory of history was the Hegelian one with classes substituted for nations. Some present-day critics of Marxism take this view, and Lenin, as well as the dialectical materialists of Eastern Europe and China, emphasize the Hegelian features of Marx's historical materialism. Marx himself, however, vacillated in his attitude towards Hegel. Like Feuerbach, he rejected Hegel's idealism. On his view, it was not spirit that moved history, but economic and industrial processes. He rejected philosophical speculation, and sought to make the study of history scientific rather than philosophical. A letter which Marx wrote to Engels on 14th January, 1858 is sometimes referred to as showing Marx's admiration for Hegel, but, while it shows that Hegel's *Logic* was at that time of interest to him, it shows that he also had serious doubts about it. Marx returned to the topic of Hegel in the Preface to the second edition of *Capital* in 1873. Here Marx addresses himself to a positivist critic of *Capital* who, in the *Revue Positiviste* had reproached him for "having treated economics metaphysically". Marx defends himself against this by quoting from other reviewers of *Capital* who had described his work as employing "the deductive method of the whole English school" and as "analytical". Marx then considers a long passage from a St. Petersburg journal which he reports as saying:

that my method of investigation is strictly realist, but that my method of exposition is unfortunately German-dialectical.

Marx then goes on to say that nevertheless this journal had given a good account of his attitude towards the study of society. The review had emphasized the following aspects of Marx's view: that he was seeking not only for the laws of social phenomena of a given period, but also of "the laws of their change"; that social orders follow one another in necessary sequences; that social change is a "natural-historical process" going on independently of the wills of individual men; that "the laws of economic life" are not the same in all societies, but that "every historical period has its own laws"; that human society proceeds according to different laws from those prevailing in animal and vegetable organisms; that types of human society grow, flourish and decline; that the dead societies are replaced by "other, higher ones". Having quoted all this, Marx then says:

When the writer describes what he calls my method so aptly, and, so far as my application of it is concerned, so generously, what else has he described but the dialectical method?

If this is so, what *is* the dialectical method here described? It is like Hegel's in its emphasis on change and on struggle and on the development of new and superior social orders. It is also like Hegel's in that it regards human societies as different in nature from biological organisms. It differs from Hegel's in treating social change as a "natural-historical process". It differs from Hegel's, too, in claiming to foresee, not only that the present social order will decline and disappear, but also that it will be replaced by a specific type of social order, that of communism. According to Marx, he had developed "the rational kernel" of that dialectical method which in Hegel's writings was a form of "mystification". The paragraph with which he ends this Preface shows what Marx had chiefly in mind:

The contradictory movement in capitalist society makes itself most strongly felt by the practical bourgeois in the vicissitudes of the periodical cycles to which modern industry is subject, and in their climax—universal crisis. Such a crisis is again on the way, although it is only in its preliminary phases. By the universality of its appearance on the scene and the intensity of its effects it will bludgeon itself into the heads of the playboys of the new, holy Prussian-German Empire.

4   Profit and Exploitation

§1   *Socialism and the Theory of Value*

Marx's and Engels' most interesting and important contribution to the understanding of history and society is undoubtedly their theory of historical materialism. They themselves, however, and their followers, have attached great importance to the theory of exchange value that Marx set out in a number of writings, notably in *Towards a Critique of Political Economy* (1859) and in *Capital*, Volume I (1867). Like several earlier attempts by Marx to expound a comprehensive theory of human society, neither of these works was completed. After Marx's death Engels arranged the publication of Volumes II (1885) and III (1894) of *Capital* from manuscripts left behind by Marx, and later on some chapters entitled *Theories of Surplus Value*, containing material that might have been intended for a fourth volume, were published by Karl Kautsky in 1905–10. It was only after the commencement of his association with Engels that Marx turned his attention to economic theory. He then made himself acquainted with the so-called classical economics of his day, as propounded by Adam Smith, J.-B. Say, Malthus and Ricardo, and by their many disciples. In developing his own economic views Marx constantly had in mind John Stuart Mill's *Principles of Political Economy* (1st edition, 1848) and Nassau Senior's work with the same title which had appeared in 1825.

An assumption of the classical economists was that their theories were universal in scope, applying to any society in which wealth is produced. Central to their theories was the notion of value. David Ricardo, the most influential of the economists of the generation after Adam Smith, wrote in the first edition of his *Principles of Political Economy and Taxation* (1817), that for anything to have exchange value, it must first have utility or use value, for if no one wanted an article no one would want to exchange anything for it either. But not everything that has utility has exchange value, for such things as air and water which can be had in abundance have no exchange value although they are useful, indeed necessary, to those who enjoy them. In order to possess exchange value, therefore, commodities must have two further features: they must be scarce and they must be products of human labour. Some objects, such as rare statues and books, obtain their value from their scarcity alone but "by far the greatest part of those goods which are the objects of desire, are procured by labour".

Ricardo went on to argue that it is "the quantity of labour realized in commodities" which is "the foundation

Profit was, according to Ricardo, the return necessary to secure a supply of capital and to make it worthwhile to the capitalist to go to the trouble and risk of providing it. Just as wages tend towards the subsistence level, so profits naturally tend to fall. "The farmer and manufacturer can no more live without profit, than the labourer without wages." Profits then, are essential features of the system which Ricardo was endeavouring to understand and to explain.

Ricardo indeed set out to *understand* the workings of the economic system rather than to criticize or justify it. In fulfilling this task, he came to see that labour is a commodity with a price, and that money and capital have prices too. The labourer's wage is what it costs to produce and maintain him, just as profit is what it costs to get a supply of capital and to maintain and replace it, and interest is what it costs to get a loan of money. In working out his theoretical scheme, Ricardo tells us that he assumed a competitive system with private property. Coolly and drily he drew the consequences involved in it. He saw that more and better machinery might increase the general prosperity, but he was by no means exuberant in his optimism. He thought it was the increase of wealth and capital which, by raising the demand for labour, had most prospect of raising wages. He thought that wage bargains, like all others, should "be left to the fair and free competition of the market". Poor-law relief, therefore, in so far as it went against this principle, was bad. The Poor Laws had "rendered restraint superfluous, and have invited imprudence, by offering it a portion of the wages of prudence and industry", and therefore they should be gradually contracted "by impressing on the poor the

of the exchangeable value of all things, excepting
which cannot be increased by human industry".
Ricardo expressed himself in terms of the so
Labour Theory of Value, a view which was widely ac
by other economists of the time, although histor
economics today suggest that Ricardo had a (
Production Theory of value rather than a Labour 7
According to the labour theory of value, capi
stored labour: if, for example, a man hunts an anim
a spear, then if he succeeds in killing it, its
equivalent to the labour of hunting and the
necessary to make the spear for that purpose
example was given by Ricardo but he also gives
realistic example: "the exchangeable value" of a
stockings, he held, depends upon the labour
growing the cotton, and in conveying the cotto
country of manufacture, the labour of the spir
weaver, the labour of the retail dealer, and a pr
of the labour of those who built the factory and s
so on.

According to this sort of theory, wages are
paid for labour, and wages tend to approxima
"price which is necessary to enable the labou
with another, to subsist and to perpetuate tl
without either increase or diminution". If the
for labour increases, the supply remaining
wages increase; if the demand falls, the supply
the same, wages fall; but these movements ten
what it costs to enable workers to live and w
standard of life which is customary at the ti
Ricardo held that wages, by and large, were
whatever was necessary for the subsistence of th

value of independence, by teaching them that they must look not to systematic or casual charity, but to their own exertions for support".

It is not surprising that these views met with opposition from socialist writers. The labour theory of value provided them with one line of criticism. Why, it was asked, should capitalists receive anything at all if labour is the source of all value? If labour is the source of all value, then labour should receive the whole of what it produces, without the intervention of landlords and capitalists. Esther Lowenthal in her book, *The Ricardian Socialists* (1911), has summarized the arguments used. The general idea was that for the capitalist to receive more than a wage for the actual work he has done in managing his firm is a trick played upon the workmen. We have seen that Engels, in his 1844 *Critique of Political Economy*, had said that the whole system in which labour was a market commodity was "a brotherhood of thieves". Marx believed that he could show that the most pessimistic of Ricardo's fears were inevitable features of the capitalist system. He thought he could show, indeed, that the system was even more dismal (to use Carlyle's word) than Ricardo himself had believed, and that within it wages must be kept low, small capitalists must be forced into bankruptcy, and monopoly must prevail. Profits were a trick and a cheat, but an inextricable and unavoidable part of the capitalist system. Nothing therefore could be done to improve the system itself. The only way to stop the cheating was to abolish the system altogether.

§2 *Surplus Value and Exploitation*

What, then, is this trick which, according to Marx, is

inexorably played against the wage-earner in the capitalist system? We have seen that Marx regarded it as Ricardo's view that labour is the source of exchange value. In enlarging on this Marx concluded that the values of commodities are, by and large, determined by the amount of "socially necessary labour" incorporated in them. But if this is so, how could an employer make a profit by selling goods at prices determined by the labour put into them by the men working to produce them for him? Or we may put the question this way. The value of the commodity produced by the workman for his employer comprises the labour contributed and incorporated in the commodity by the workman plus the labour stored in the machines he uses and transferred to the commodity he produces with their help. This being so, how could it profit any capitalist to go into business? What advantage is there for him in this process of incorporating value, that is labour, into commodities which, by and large, sell at prices which represent this value? Marx's answer to this question is as follows.

What the worker sells to the capitalist is not merely the labour he incorporates into the commodities he makes but his labour *power*, his *ability* to work and produce, and the capitalist pays for this labour power by agreeing to a rate of wages. The worker's labour power, since it is bought and sold, is a commodity, and as a commodity it has value. This value, according to Marx, consists in the labour necessary to maintain the worker and enable him to reproduce his kind. Since things tend to exchange for their value, the employer pays his workers those amounts of money which enable them to obtain their subsistence. That is, he pays them wages that enable them to buy the amounts of food and drink and housing that will keep them and their families going. According to Marx's labour theory of value, the value of the worker's labour power is the amount of labour socially necessary to produce the worker's subsistence. Amounts of labour are measured by the time spent labouring, so that the subsistence of the worker has as its value the hours of work socially necessary to secure it. Marx reasoned that the capitalist is able to strike a bargain with the wage-earner which requires the latter to work for a longer period than is necessary in order to secure his subsistence. That is, according to Marx, the capitalist can get the wage-earner to give him more value than the real value of the work done. To this extra value Marx gave the name surplus value. It is from this surplus value, he argued, that industrialists and merchants get their profits, bankers and other money-lenders their interest, and landowners their rent. This is how the essential fraud of capitalism is effected. Capitalism would be impossible without surplus value and is hence, in its very nature, a system of exploitation. Exploitation is simply the obtaining of surplus value, the extraction from the worker of more value than he really costs the capitalist. It is not merely that some capitalists sometimes exploit their workers, but rather that all capitalists necessarily exploit their workers. For without profits there could be no capitalists and without surplus value and exploitation there could be no profits.

It is natural to ask how it comes about that the capitalist can induce the worker to work for more hours than is necessary to produce the value of his subsistence. Marx's main answer is as follows:

Wherever a part of society posses a monopoly of the means of production the worker, whether he is free or a slave, must add to the labour-time necessary for his own maintenance surplus labour-time in order to produce means of living for the owner of the means of production, whether this owner is an Athenian καλοκἀγαθός, an Etruscan theocrat, a Roman citizen, a Norman baron, an American shareholder, a Wallachian Boyar or a modern landlord or capitalist. (*Capital*, Vol. I, Ch. 8, §2)

It is surprising that Marx should here give examples taken from non-capitalist, as well as from capitalist, societies, but it is clear that in the passage he is saying that it is because of their monopoly position that capitalists can exploit wage-earners. Exploitation would be rendered more difficult, or even impossible, if wage-earners had not to face a monopoly of capitalists who own the means of production and hence can always get the better of the bargain.

Another point to notice in Marx's account of surplus value is that he argued that the wage-earner generally gives credit to the employer. Marx's reason for saying this is that wages are generally paid *after* the work contracted for has been done.

In all countries with the capitalist method of production, the working time is only paid for when it has functioned throughout the period specified in the contract, e.g. at the end of each week. Everywhere, therefore, the worker lends the capitalist the use-value of his labour-power; he allows the buyer to consume it before he has paid the price; thus the worker everywhere gives credit to the capitalist. (*Capital*, Vol. I, Ch. 4, §3)

It should also be noted that Marx claimed that his
account of surplus value is purely scientific, a matter of
description and analysis, rather than a moral indictment.
From many passages in which this is said or implied we
may choose the following:

It is an extraordinarily cheap form of sentimentality to
regard as coarse or brutal this method of determining the
value of labour power, which in fact arises from the nature
of the case. (*Capital*, Vol. I, Ch. 4, §3)
The daily maintenance of the labour power costs only
half a day's labour, although the labour power can work
a whole working day,

[Marx takes this as an *example* and is not suggesting that
this is the proportion that always holds.]

so that the value that its use creates during a working day
is twice the value of a day's labour power. This is fortunate
for the buyer, but is in no way an injustice against the
seller. (*Capital*, Vol. I, Ch. 5, §2)

This repudiation of moral criticism is found also in the
chapter of *Capital* entitled "The Working Day" where
Marx writes:

The capitalist upholds his right as buyer when he tries
to make the working day as long as possible, and if possible
to make two working days out of one. On the other hand,
the specific nature of the commodity that has been sold
[to him] sets a limit upon the buyer's consumption of it,
and the worker upholds his right as seller when he tries to
restrict the working day to a normal length. Thus there is
here an antinomy in which right conflicts with right and

both are hallowed by the law of the exchange of commodities. Between two equal rights it is force that decides. (*Capital*, Vol. I, Ch. 8, §1)

In these passages Marx appears to be deprecating the passing of moral judgments condemning the exploitation of the workers by the capitalists. It is sentimentality to describe it as rough or brutal, and *both* wage-earners *and* employers have right on their side. If this means that the issue can only be settled by force, this is a statement of fact and analysis, not a moral indictment. Marx seems to be refusing to appeal either to men's hearts or sympathies or to their sense of justice. Yet all this is belied by things he says elsewhere in *Capital*. For example, in Chapter 8, §5, Marx writes:

In its blind, unbridled drive, in its werewolf greed for surplus labour, capital oversteps not only the moral restrictions upon the working-day but also its purely physical limitations. It usurps the time needed for the growth, development and healthy maintenance of the body. It steals the time needed for free air and the light of the sun. . . .

Werewolves are greedy for the blood of their victims and steal it from them, so that capital, if it does the same, must be a particularly unattractive institution. Analysis and description have been supplemented by denunciation, and the profit-seeker is held to be Dracula in a rather thin disguise. Can it be, then, that all this parade of economic analysis covers, in spite of Marx's disclaimers, a moral attack upon capitalism? It seems to me that Marx's *Capital* is, in its fundamentals, such a moral condemnation.

Both in *Towards a Critique of Political Economy* and in Volume I of *Capital* Marx discusses the nature of commodities, pointing out that they have use value, for example, shoes are useful for protecting the feet of the wearer, and that they have exchange value too, as when the maker of them exchanges them for money or for some other article made by someone else. We have seen that Marx, like Ricardo before him, believed that the exchange-value of commodities represented the labour required to make them. Marx argued, both in his *Critique of Political Economy* and in *Capital* that in pre-capitalist societies which had the use of money, the exchange transactions which men entered into took the form of "the transformation of a commodity into money and the retransformation of the money into a commodity" (*Capital*, Vol. I, Ch. 4, §1). He symbolized this in the formula C-M-C, i.e., a commodity is exchanged for money and the money is then spent on buying some other commodity. The situation that Marx here calls attention to is that in which money is used as a means of exchanging goods. In such a situation it is the use-value of the commodities that matters, and money is not sought for itself but only for the things it will buy.

Marx contrasts with this plain and beneficial situation that in which money is first used to buy commodities and the commodities are then sold for money, symbolized as M-C-M. In this second type of situation, he says, money is no longer merely a means of exchange, but has become capital. In the sequence C-M-C, someone sells a commodity he is not in need of in order to acquire with the money something else he is in need of. But in the sequence M-C-M, a commodity is bought only to be sold again, and there would be no point in doing this unless the money obtained at the end exceeds that with which the operator started the series. The buyer of the commodity only parts with his money, says Marx, "with the sly purpose of getting it back again". The use of the word "sly" should put us on our guard, and Marx goes on to say that the difference between the first M in the sequence and the last M is "surplus value". Capital necessarily implies surplus value and surplus value is something which sly men seek. These men are not concerned with the things that money will buy but with money itself. They are unnatural men, veritable werewolves.

In this part of the argument Marx refers at some length to Aristotle's *Politics*, Book I, Ch. 9, where Aristotle distinguishes between the art of household management ("economics") and the art of acquisition ("chrematistic"). Aristotle there argued that it is right and natural to acquire goods by one's own productive effort or by purchase, with a view to using them in the proper purposes of life. On the other hand there is a sort of acquisition which has as its object merely the making of money. Commercial activities which have the acquisition of useful objects as their end are limited activities that cease when human needs are provided for. But those commercial activities which have money-making as their object are unlimited and have no natural terminus. Reasonable needs can be satisfied, whereas money can be, and is, sought for *ad infinitum*. Hunger can be satisfied but the desire for money has no end. From this it is quite clear that the sequence that Marx labels C-M-C is the kind of economic activity, with money as a *means* of exchange only, that Aristotle thought was morally justified, while the sequence M-C-M is the *unnatural* chrematistic which Aristotle condemned. Aristotle's views on this matter were influential in medieval Europe and were used as arguments against charging interest for loans of money. Strange as it may seem in the light of his own disclaimers, what Marx did was to revive or reformulate the Aristotelian and medieval arguments so as to condemn capitalism as the form of society in which the endless and infinite search for money perverted the life of the community. Marx writes:

> The capitalist knows that all commodities, however shabby they look and however badly they smell, are in faith and in truth money, are inwardly circumcized Jews, and at the same time a wonderful means of making more money from money. (*Capital*, Vol. I, Ch. 4, §1)

Marx here coarsely identifies profit-seekers with Jews, as he had already done in *On the Jewish Question* (1844). The difference between Marx's attitude towards profit and the medieval moralists' attitude towards usury is that the latter sought to prevent usury without bringing about a social revolution, whereas Marx held that profit and exploitation are essential features of capitalism and can only be abolished by abolishing capitalism itself. According to Marx, in capitalistic society the M-C-M sequence predominates over the C-M-C sequence, the bad form of chrematistic over the justifiable form of trade and economy, the insatiable search for the unrealizable over moderation and stability. When we have grasped this we see that his tortuous and obsolete economic reasoning is a rather unimportant decoration, or perhaps even a rather modest drapery, which conceals what is fundamentally a moral analysis in the Aristotelian or Thomist style.

A further aspect of Marx's view which should be noticed is that he held that the classical economists were wrong in supposing that the economic laws which they claimed to have discovered held for all human societies. At the end of Chapter 3 I called attention to what Marx thought was involved in his dialectical method, and one feature of it was that different forms of society had different economic laws. Marx believed that capitalist society had economic laws of its own different from those of pre-capitalist society. In a sense he was right, in the sense, namely, that the production of goods for sale so predominates in capitalist society over production for immediate use that profit and saleability occupy a special and dominating place in it. Marx wished to conclude, of course, that a form of society into which profit did not enter was not only possible but was certain to emerge. He did not consider, however, whether there are principles about the least wasteful allocation of scarce resources which must apply to any economic system, socialist and non-socialist alike. The Classical Economists were hasty in concluding that they knew what these principles are, but if Marx intended to deny that there are any he was too hasty himself.

§3 *Some Inherent Defects of Capitalism*

Marx thought he could show that the capitalist system not only necessitated the exploitation of the workers by their employers but contained inescapable internal "antagonisms". One of these consisted in the tendency towards increased poverty among the workers as the size and power of capital was augmented. Linked with this "Law of Increasing Misery" is the occurrence of periodical economic crises in the course of which workers lose their jobs and are only too pleased to return to work on terms dictated to them by the capitalists. Marx believed that capitalism required for its working an "industrial reserve army" of unemployed men. The defenders of capitalism said that when new capital came into use there was an increased demand for the labour-power to work it. According to Marx, however, any advantage that this might secure for those who got the new jobs was nullified by the pressure upon them of those who are out of work:

... the pressure of the unemployed on the employed compels the employed to busy themselves in supplying more labour, and thus, in a certain degree, makes the supply of labour independent of the supply of workers. (*Capital*, Vol. I, Ch. 23, §3)

The only way in which this "despotism of capital" could be lessened would be by co-operation between employed and unemployed workers in trades unions.

But where does this "industrial reserve army" come from? First, there are those thrown out of work by "the changing phases of the industrial cycle, so that unemployment is acute during the crisis and chronic in times of slack trade". Then there are those who change their jobs, those who are dismissed because of their age, and those who enter the labour market as children. There is also, according to Marx, a body of surplus workers always ready to leave the rural areas, and those whose jobs are irregular or who are not fit for uninterrupted employment. Marx concludes:

The greater the social wealth, the functioning capital, extent and energy of its growth, and the greater therefore the absolute size of the proletariat and the productive force of its work, the greater the reserve army. The available labour-power has its extent advanced by the same causes as those which advance the expansive force of capital. Therefore, the relative magnitude of the industrial reserve army increases as wealth increases. But the larger this reserve army is in relation to the active labour army, the larger is the mass of the consolidated surplus population, whose poverty is in inverse relation to the anguish of its labour. Finally the larger the Lazarus stratum of the working class and the industrial reserve army, the larger too becomes official pauperism. *This is the absolute law of capitalist accumulation.* Like all other laws, it is modified in its realization by numerous circumstances, the analysis of which would not be in place here. (*Capital*, Vol. I, Ch. 23, §4)

A little later in the same section Marx writes:

The accumulation of wealth at one pole of society is at the same time an accumulation of distress, of anguish in labour, slavery, ignorance, brutalization and moral degradation at the opposite pole, that is, on the side of the class that produces its own product in the form of capital.

We saw in Chapter 1, §3 that quite early in the nineteenth century Sismondi and Malthus had called attention to industrial crises and had suggested that a cause of them was that the working classes had insufficient money to buy all the products of capitalist industry. That is, they had called attention to the possibility of under-consumption. Sismondi had urged the payment of higher wages so as to increase the demand in that way. Malthus had tentatively suggested public works and had also suggested it would help if some classes went in for luxury spending. Marx was aware of these discussions but, although he agreed that there was under-consumption, he rejected the proposed remedies. In Chapter XIX of *Theories of Surplus Value*, the unpublished manuscript that he had hoped to complete as the fourth Volume of *Capital*, he was particularly critical of Malthus' advocacy of luxury spending. Indeed, like most socialists, he detested Malthus, whose *Essay on the Principle of Population* (1798) had been first written in order to show that increasing population was likely to counteract the benefits of social reform. (Marx's dislike for "Parson Malthus" was extended to "other Protestant Parsons who have shuffled off the Catholic command of celibacy of the clergy and have taken the motto 'Be fruitful and multiply', as their specific biblical mission with such success that they everywhere contribute to the increase of the population in a quite unbecoming degree, while at the same time they preach 'the principle of population' to the workers". This is only part of an extremely abusive footnote near the beginning of *Capital*, Vol. I, Ch. 23.) It was only natural that Marx should be suspicious of Malthus' theories, and he had no sympathy for any suggestions for removing the evils from capitalism and trying to improve its working. For he denied that it *could* be improved. Surplus value was essential to it, this was exploitation, exploitation must get worse and worse, the dread capitalist werewolf must have his blood.

Unemployment, poverty and pauperization—these, Marx wrote, are "the absolute law of capitalist accumulation". Somewhat inconsistently he also wrote that this, like all other laws, is subject to modification. But he can hardly have expected that in capitalist economies unemployment would be lessened or abolished, poverty diminished and the majority of workers rendered prosperous if not contented. Of course, the capitalism within which these things have been done is not the *laissez-faire* capitalism that Marx was analysing. Nevertheless it is capitalism in the sense that a large part of the commerce and industry that goes on in it is carried out with a view to profit. Increased profits and increased capitalization have not led to more poverty but to less. The ideas of Sismondi and of Malthus have been revived and developed and applied so as to even out trade cycles to some extent and to lessen the amount of unemployment. The application of these policies has brought problems with it, of course, as the diminution of unemployment beyond a certain point now presents *labour* with a monopoly which society finds it hard to cope with. [1] In *Capital* Marx was analysing and stigmatizing a form of society that no longer exists, and even if his indictment of it were to be accepted, it would not be applicable or even relevant to the society in which we live, which has faults of quite a different order.

5 Revolution, the State and the Communist Ideal

§1 *The Coming Catastrophe*

We have seen that Marx took over from Saint-Simon the idea that a social system contains within itself the "germ of its own destruction" which is at the same time the growing-point of a new social order which will supersede it. Marx believed that the capitalist order of society was divided by irreconcilable antagonisms, of which the clash of rights between worker and employer was the principal. Like Hegel before him, Marx held that when two rights clash, the issue must be settled by force. Furthermore, if the workers must get poorer and poorer, they will be provoked to violence by despair. Marx also believed that the profits of individual capitalists and firms must increasingly diminish and that because of the increasing poverty of the workers, markets would shrink and goods remain unsold. Intensified competition between capitalists would drive the weaker ones out of business and into the ranks of the proletariat, while those that survived would concentrate their forces and set up monopolies. The whole system was then bound to come to an end in a welter of economic crises, trade disputes, bankruptcies and universal confusion. At this point, Marx believed, the workers would rise against the system of capitalist private property and bring it to an end.

One capitalist finishes off many capitalists. Hand in hand with this centralization or the expropriation of many capitalists by a few, the co-operative form of the labour-process evolves in ever-increasing stages. There is a conscious application of science to technology, a planned exploitation of the earth, the transformation of instruments of labour into instruments of labour that can only be used in common, economies of all the means of production through using them as means of production in joint, social labour. All the peoples are enmeshed in the network of the world market so that the capitalist regime assumes an international character. With the constantly diminishing number of the capitalist magnates who usurp and monopolize all the advantages of this transformative process, there is an increase in the mass of distress, oppression, bondage, degeneration, exploitation. But there is also a rising of the working class, who will have been constantly growing in numbers and are schooled, united and organized through the working of the capitalist process of production. The monopoly of capital becomes a brake on the method of production which has flourished with it and under it. Centralization of the means of production and socialization of labour reach a point at which they are incompatible with the capitalist integument.

This bursts asunder. The hour of capitalist private property strikes. The expropriators are expropriated. (*Capital*, Vol. I, Ch. 24, §7)

This was published in 1867, and Marx did not regard it as a very long-term prophecy. Like those early Christians who expected Christ to return in glory any day, Marx thought that the capitalism of his time would explode and be replaced by a new order. It was only after the failure and suppression of the Paris Commune in 1871 that Marx's hopes of a speedy transformation began to fade. The ultimate hope, of course, remained, and was transmitted to his followers, many of whom still cherish it. But a hundred years after these words were published a modified capitalism still remains, taking different forms in different countries. Poverty has not increased. Profits continue to be obtained, though they are heavily taxed. Capitalist enterprises expand and merge with one another, sometimes at the promptings of governments elected by working class voters. But small new enterprises constantly enter the system, some failing, others going on to expand and prosper. As Marx predicted, scientific discoveries are increasingly applied in the industrial field. But trades unions now have a lot of influence in deciding when and how rapidly these applications can be made. Socialized and co-operative methods of production have not so far proved incompatible with capitalist private property. Indeed, the ownership of shares has spread and unit trusts have made it possible for many more people to participate in the ownership of trade and industry. But, again as Marx predicted, the association of workers in large industries has led them to form cohesive groups. But Marx did not predict that when the workers work shorter hours, the employments of their leisure take on an added importance. Taking part in sport and watching it, give rise to different loyalties. Motoring tends to tighten the family bond and to encourage individual pursuits and explorations. The coexistence of capitalism with universal suffrage and competing political parties has shifted power towards organized labour and has encouraged hostility towards employers without discouraging the pursuit of private advantage. If collapse and catastrophe do take place, they are as likely to result from too much consumption and too little labour injudiciously deployed, as from underconsumption and overwork.

§2 *Organizing the Workers*

In 1864 Marx was active in the formation of the International Working-men's Association, the so-called First International. This had its headquarters in London, and Marx and his French and German associates had to get the support of the less revolutionary English tradeunionists. Among concrete reforms for which the Association worked was the legal restriction of the length of the working day. Marx, of course, looked upon this as an attempt to limit the amount of surplus value which the capitalist could extort from the worker, but some of his English associates just regarded it as a means of bettering the condition of their members within a system which they did not question in any fundamental way. Marx actually wrote the Inaugural Address. It is interesting to read Marx's account of how he came to do this. In a letter to Engels dated 4th November, 1864 Marx says that Cremer (an English carpenter who later became a Liberal Member of Parliament), Fontana (an Italian) and Le Lubez, met in Marx's house bringing various papers and drafts with them which Marx had not hitherto seen. Marx immediately decided "that if possible not one single line of the stuff should be allowed to stand".

In order to gain time, I proposed: before we "edited" the preamble, we should "discuss" the rules. That is what happened. It was one o'clock in the morning before the first of the forty rules was accepted. Cremer said (*and that is what I had planned*): we have nothing to put before the Committee that meets on 25th October. We must put it off until 1st November. Then the sub-committee can meet on the 27th October and try to reach a definite conclusion. This was agreed and the "papers" "left" for me to look over. I saw it impossible to make anything out of the stuff.

Marx goes on to say that at the sub-committee all his proposals were accepted.

Except that I was obliged to include in the preamble to the rules two phrases about "duty" and "right", ditto "truth, morality and justice", which, however, are so placed that they can't do any harm.

Then Marx's "Address, etc. was accepted by the General Committee with great enthusiasm (unanimously)". Further on in the letter Marx wrote:

It was very difficult to keep things so that our view appeared in a form that made it acceptable to the present standpoint of the workers' movement. In a few weeks the same people will be holding meetings for the franchise with Bright and Cobden. It needs time before the reawakened movement allows the old boldness of speech. It is necessary to be *fortiter in re, suaviter in modo.*

In 1844 Marx had said that philosophy was "the head" of the emancipation of mankind, the proletariat its "heart". The letter from which we have quoted shows how the head set about gaining control of the heart. Appeals to "truth, morality and justice" were simple-minded, and to be borne with only when necessary and then with reluctance. Cremer and workers who thought like him could be made into instruments of history by being manipulated by those who knew the direction in which history was moving.

In their valuable book, *Karl Marx and the British Labour Movement* (Macmillan, London, 1965), H. Collins and C. Abramsky describe the manoeuvres that attended the beginning of the First International, and also print some extracts from Marx's Inaugural Address, composed as a result of the methods we have just described. An important passage runs as follows:

No improvement of machinery, no appliances [sic] of science to production, no contrivances of communication, no new colonies, no emigration, no opening of markets, no free trade, nor all of these things put together, will do away with the miseries of the industrious masses; but that, on the present false base, every fresh development of the productive powers of labour must tend to deepen social contrasts and point social antagonisms.

The word "appliances" where "applications" is called for, betrays Marx's incomplete grasp of English usage. But the passage comes very close to stating the doctrine of increasing misery expounded three years later in *Capital*. Whatever Marx's readers understood by "the present false base", Marx himself meant the capitalist system with its essential connection with money, surplus value and exploitation. Thus he is saying that, as long as capitalism lasts, the gap between rich and poor must get wider and social antagonisms must get greater. This was accepted "with great enthusiasm (unanimously)" by men whose minds did not grasp its import.

§3   *Making the Revolution*

The First International came to an end in 1872, but just before this the events of the Paris Commune led to a publication of great importance for the subsequent development of Marxist socialism, Marx's *The Civil War in France*, the first edition of which appeared in June, 1871, in English. It was published at twopence a copy and described as "Address of the General Council of the International Working-men's Association". The members of the General Council listed in the pamphlet had such English names as Boon and Bradick, but the "Corresponding Secretary" for Germany and Holland was Karl Marx and that for Belgium and Spain was Friedrich Engels. After the defeat of France in the Franco-Prussian War of 1870–1, a revolutionary government had seized power in Paris and proclaimed itself the government of France. Many of its leaders were socialists of one kind or another, and the troops of the defeated government, with Thiers as Prime Minister, laid siege to Paris and after a few weeks entered Paris and put down the Commune with great bloodshed. While they had power the regime of the Commune had destroyed important monuments and had shot a number of hostages among whom was Darboy, the Archbishop of Paris.

Many who sympathized with socialist aims were shocked by these events, even though they were also shocked by the executions which took place when the regular troops regained control of Paris. But Marx was full of enthusiasm for the Commune, which he regarded as the first attempt to form a working-class government. He expressed approval of the fact that this government was not a parliament, but a body which combined legislative and executive functions. He noted with satisfaction that the members of this government were paid workmen's wages, that they got rid of the army and police force that had served the previous government, that they disestablished and disendowed all churches and sent the priests back into private life, that they had judges elected by the people and revocable by them, that they abolished certain forms of night work and prohibited fines by employers on their workpeople, that they encouraged associations of workmen to take over workshops and factories. The shooting of hostages which had caused such widespread condemnation was justified by Marx:

How could they be spared any longer after the bloodbath with which MacMahon's praetorians were celebrating their march into Paris? Would it have been right for the last counterpoise against the relentless savagery of the bourgeois governments—the seizing of hostages—to become nothing but a mockery? The real murderer of Bishop Darboy is Thiers. The Commune had repeatedly offered to exchange the Archbishop and a whole heap of priests against Blanqui, the only one held by Thiers. Thiers obstinately refused. He knew that with Blanqui he would be giving the Commune a head, while the Archbishop would serve his purpose best as a corpse.

The Blanqui here referred to was a revolutionary socialist who had taken part in the revolutions of 1830 and 1848 and who advocated and took part in conspiratorial preparations for taking over power, rather in the tradition of Baboeuf. Blanqui outlived the Archibishop by ten years.

It is not surprising that Marx's pamphlet aroused a great deal of indignation, much of it ill-informed, against the International Working-men's Association on whose behalf it had been issued. Indeed, it caused dissension within the International itself which soon afterwards moved to the United States and petered out there. But the pamphlet itself later became an important source of Marxist socialist doctrine. Marx did not merely excuse the Commune's use of violence, but positively gloried in it. He propounded the view that it would be harmful if the revolutionary workers accepted the existing state power and expected that they could operate it on their own behalf. The Central Committee of the Commune had written of "seizing the governmental power", but Marx said that "the working class cannot simply seize the ready-made state machinery and use it for its own purposes". Writing (a little earlier) to a German admirer, Dr. Kugelmann, Marx had said that "the next attempt of the French revolution will be no longer, as before, to transfer the bureaucratic military machine from one hand to another, but to smash it . . ." (letter to Kugelmann,

12th April, 1871). The army and civil service of the bourgeois regime was not, in Marx's view, a neutral apparatus ready to work on behalf of whoever occupied supreme power. On the contrary, the bourgeois police, bourgeois officials and bourgeois army were instruments of bourgeois class rule and would have to be replaced by armed men and administrators from the working class.

By writing in these terms, Marx made it clear how very different his outlook was from the outlook of those who supported parliamentary democracy. In a parliamentary democracy a new government is voted in and has at its disposal the officials and police and army which had previously served the government that had been voted out. What Marx looked forward to was a violent attack on the state apparatus itself and its replacement by a new form of state acting directly on behalf of the working classes and appointed by them to protect their interests against any attempts by the capitalists to re-establish themselves. This idea was later developed, notably by Lenin, into the Communist Party doctrine of the "dictatorship of the proletariat". In the *Critique of the Gotha Programme* Marx himself says that when capitalist society is being transformed into communist society there will be "a political transition period in which the state can be nothing but *the revolutionary dictatorship of the proletariat*". But it should be noticed that, although Marx advocated the destruction of the old state organization and the use of violence, he also approved of the fact that the leaders of the Commune were "chosen by universal suffrage in various sections of the city and responsible and revocable at short terms" (*The Civil War in France*).

He seems to have believed that insurrection and violence by and on behalf of the proletariat were consistent, even while the violence continued, with popular democratic control. He may well have over-simplified the possibilities, for what happened during a local and short-lived uprising like that of the Paris Commune is not likely to be a useful precedent for a revolution on a national scale.

Marx believed, then, that the working classes should be encouraged to agitate against the conditions imposed on them by their employers. He believed, too, that trade union leaders should be enlisted in the cause of revolutionary socialism, willingly if they accepted the aim, unknowingly if they did not. He expected that the revolution, when it came, would be violent and perhaps bloody, because its success would depend upon "smashing" the state that was manned and organized to uphold the class domination of the capitalists.

We must now consider what Marx thought would be the outcome of all this, what benefits would be secured, what form of life would emerge.

§4 *The Post-revolutionary Social Order*

In his *Utopia* (1516), Sir Thomas More gave an account of an imaginary society from which luxury and greed had been banished. His idea in doing this was to bring out the contrast between this good form of society that might be and the existing society in which some men were overworked and undernourished and others lived in idle luxury. Since More wrote his *Utopia*, critics and reformers have imagined all sorts of ideal societies, and the adjective "utopian" has come to be applied to social schemes and visions of the future which are far removed from practical possibility. Some of the socialist writers known to Marx and Engels at the beginning of their careers were Utopian socialists in this sense. In *The Communist Manifesto* there is a section headed "Critical-utopian Socialism and Communism" in which Marx and Engels wrote of "fantastic pictures of future society" and "duodecimo editions of the New Jerusalem". It was their view that writers such as Fourier who described in detail the form of life and society they looked forward to belonged to the earliest, pre-scientific phase of socialism. Utopian socialists, Marx and Engels believed, failed to realize the extent of the class division and class conflict that was essential to capitalist society, and hence they hoped to enlist support for their schemes from bourgeois philanthropists and to set up socialist societies in the midst of capitalism, without disarming and destroying it. In so far as their descriptions of socialist societies to come asserted or implied criticisms of the existing social order, Utopian socialists were to be applauded. But in so far as they hoped that once their schemes for an ideal society were understood and accepted, mankind would hasten to carry them out, the Utopian socialists were not only themselves deceived but were sources of deception for their followers. Because, therefore, they rejected Utopian socialism, Marx and Engels did not have much to say about the details of the society they aimed to establish. They often preferred, in consequence, to use the term "communism" for the *movement* which would overcome the capitalist order, rather than for the society that would ultimately emerge. An example of this usage occurs in *The German Ideology*, where they say:

Communism is not for us a condition which ought to be established, an *ideal* to which reality will have to conform itself. We call communism the *real* movement which abolishes the present condition.

Nevertheless, it would not have been reasonable or even possible for Marx and Engels to remain completely silent about the socialism or communism of the future. At the very least it must be describable in negative terms, as non-capitalism and post-capitalism, that is, as a non-capitalist social order which is an *advance* on capitalism and not a mere reversion to an earlier type of society. One feature of it, clearly, will be that in it there will be no capitalist class owning the means of production. There will indeed, be no classes at all, since the proletariat, the great mass of the population, will, after its triumph, dissolve all class distinctions. Another feature of it will be that production and distribution will not be carried out competitively, as under capitalism, but will be publicly organized with the object of satisfying the needs of all. It will be need rather than money demand that will keep the economic and industrial system in motion. We have already seen Engels' statement of this at the end of Chapter 1, §3, in the passage we have quoted from his *Sketch of a Critique of Political Economy*, where he suggests that the requirements of consumers would be ascertained and the production of goods organized accordingly. In *The Communist Manifesto* there is a vaguer statement that "all production" will be "concentrated in the hands of a vast association of the whole nation" and a still vaguer one that there will be "an association in which the free development of each is the condition for the free development of all".

We pointed out in Chapter 1, however, that *The Communist Manifesto* was worked up from a catechism about communism which Engels had written and had given to Marx. This catechism, which is called *Fundamental Principles of Communism*, is more explicit than the *Manifesto* itself about the general features of the communist society of the future. Question Twenty of the catechism is: "What will be the consequence of the final removal of private property?" Engels gives a lengthy answer to this question. He says that society will remove "the employment of all productive forces and instruments of commerce from the hands of private capitalists and use them in accordance with a plan based on existing means and on the needs of the whole society". This is nothing but a rephrasing of the passage from Engels' *Sketch of a Critique of Political Economy* which he had written in 1843. The use of the word "plan", however, assimilates it, to some extent, with the conception of a "planned economy" so dear to the political leaders of our own day. Engels continues, however, in the following manner:

Just as the peasants and handworkers of the previous century altered their whole way of life and became quite different men when they were dragged into large-scale industry, so quite different men will be needed and will be created when production is carried out in common by society as a whole and when production accordingly develops in new ways.

Engels goes on:

When industry is conducted in common and in accordance with plans determined by the whole of society, it presupposes men whose dispositions are developed on all sides, who are in a position to take a view of the whole system of production. The division of labour—now already being undermined by machines—which makes one man a farmer, another a shoemaker, another a factory worker, another a Stock Exchange speculator, will therefore vanish completely. Education will enable young people to experience the whole system of production; it will put them in a position to pass over in sequence from one branch of production to another, according as the needs of society or their own inclinations require. Thus education will take away from them the one-sided character which the division of labour now impresses upon every individual. In this way, society organized communistically will give its members the opportunity of bringing into many-sided activity their many-sidedly developed dispositions. Thereupon the different classes will necessarily vanish. On the one hand, therefore, a society organized in the communist manner is incompatible with the maintenance of classes, and on the other hand, the establishing of this sort of society itself offers the means of getting rid of the distinctions between classes.

Communist society, then, will be a society of many-sided men engaged, each one of them, in many types of activity. In pre-communist societies men are forced to become specialists, and thus their spheres of activity are limited. This means that they are forced to become limited men, men who can only do one or two things out of the enormous range of possible things. Engels seems to think that as machine-production develops, each individual will be enabled, given the training, to pass from one type of job to another. A farmer can only live a farmer's life, a shoemaker only the life of a shoemaker, but when large-scale production is organized along communist lines, in terms of an agreed plan, individuals can be educated so as to switch from one type of job to another and so to develop all the different sides of their nature instead of only one or two. From what Engels says it is not clear precisely *how* this could happen. It might be thought that if there were no division of labour and no class differences, society would be *more* uniform than before. Engels' point is, however, that with the abolition of classes and of the division of labour, no man is held down to one type of life, whether it be that of a farmer or of a domestic servant or man of wealth, but can develop all the abilities he naturally possesses and not merely those that his job or his class force upon him. The division of labour and the distinctions between classes diversify *society* but place limitations upon *individuals*. When all men are placed on one level and can plan production in terms of need, then it is open to anyone to turn his hand to anything. Engels appears to be arguing that when society is divided into classes, individual lives are limited, and that when there are no classes, each individual can develop all his powers and is hence as free from limitation as it is possible to be.

Nearly thirty years later Marx himself discussed the nature of post-capitalist society in his *Critique of the Gotha Programme* (1875). The occasion of this long letter or memorandum was a document drawn up in an attempt to bring together the two German socialist parties, one of which claimed to support the views of Marx and Engels and the other those of Ferdinand Lassalle. By the time Marx wrote these comments he was a tired and disappointed man, and they contain passages that are angrily unconstructive. The writers of the programme had called for a "just distribution" of the proceeds of labour, and Marx, in the manner we have already referred to, says that the existing distribution was "just" in terms of the capitalist system itself. He then goes on to say that in the initial stages of communist society, it must bear the marks of the capitalist society from which it has emerged. The principle of distribution, therefore, must have some resemblance to that which had prevailed before the means of production had been taken from capitalist control. The point of resemblance is that the workers would be paid equal rates for equal hours of work. "The same quantity of labour which he has given to society in one form he receives back in another." But when this principle is used, then inequalities are set up, in that, when two men are paid the same for the same amounts of labour, one may be better off because he has no children, another because he is stronger and is not so easily tired, and so on. Equal pay for equal work, therefore, Marx points out, can lead to inequalities. Furthermore, when this principle is applied, men are regarded as workers only, not as individual men with specific individual needs.

Marx then gives a brief indication of what he calls "a higher phase of communist society", the phase reached when the traces of capitalism have disappeared.

In a higher phase of communist society, when the enslaving subordination of the individual to the division of labour, and therewith also the antithesis between mental and physical labour, has vanished, when labour has become not only a means of life but life's prime need; when the productive forces have also increased with the many-sided development of the individual, and all the

springs of associative wealth flow more abundantly—
only then can the narrow horizon of bourgeois right be
completely transcended and society inscribe on its banner:
"From each according to his ability, to each according to
his needs".

It will be seen that Marx, like Engels, looked forward to
a form of society in which individuals could develop as
many sides of their nature as possible. In communist
society men would not be condemned to one-sided and
limited careers through having to fall in with the division
of labour and with barriers between classes. There would
no longer be a division between men who work with their
minds and men who work with their hands. It would be
open to anyone to go in for anything, and in consequence,
Marx believed, industry would be more productive. Then
it would be possible for each individual to contribute his
best to the common task, and to receive in return whatever
he needed in order to do so. He would no longer be
rewarded as a worker, but would be sustained in accordance with his individual requirements. He would not be
an abstract item on a payroll but a concrete member of a
united community. Work would no longer be an imposed
task but the realization of individual human achievement.
It is interesting to notice in this connection that Marx did
not think that child labour should be universally prohibited. He believed, of course, that working hours
should be strictly limited, but he thought that some
proportion of child labour was essential to large-scale
industry and that its general prohibition was "a pious
hope". Moreover, he believed that it should be positively
encouraged in so far as it enabled children to receive a
suitable education at their place of work. I rather think

that Marx would have regarded the sharp separation between work and leisure that is characteristic of our times as an instance of that division and shattering of the unified individual which are the baleful consequences of class distinction and the division of labour. The newly created man who was to emerge in communist society would be many-sided but yet in harmony with himself and others.

§5 *Marxist Morality*

From what has been said so far the reader must be in some doubt as to Marx's attitude to morality and as to the moral outlook he himself had, if indeed, he had one at all. Did he, for example, regard morality as an ideology, and therefore as a form of false consciousness like religion? When he and Engels give lists of the ideologies in *The German Ideology*, they include "morality" on one occasion, and "ethics" on another, as one of the ideologies, along with religion, metaphysics, theology and philosophy, and the political ideologies. In Marx's Preface to *Towards a Critique of Political Economy*, however, neither "morality" nor "ethics" is listed, and when Engels discussed the subject of ideologies in correspondence with Conrad Schmidt in 1890, he did not mention morality either. On the other hand, both Marx and Engels wrote of legal or juridical ideologies, and it is difficult to separate law entirely from morality. Furthermore, when Marx and Engels wrote of the various ideologies, they often end their list with "etc.", so that we cannot be sure what items they intended to include. What cannot be doubted is that Marx and Engels thought that moral standards changed enormously from one historical epoch to another.

Thus in *The German Ideology* they say that when the aristocracy were dominant, honour and loyalty were leading conceptions and that when the bourgeoisie gained the ascendancy the dominant conceptions were "freedom, equality, etc." This suggests but does not demonstrate that Marx and Engels believed that moral codes and standards are determined by and relative to the basic economic and industrial organization of society, so that there is no universally authoritative set of moral standards or moral principles. It is possible that their view was the less sceptical one that men in power in different forms of society will *in fact* endeavour to justify their position by arguments that are limited in scope and devoid of cogency. Experience suggests that this is often done, but if we condemn or criticize it, we must do so in terms of standards which we regard as less limited and by means of arguments which we consider more cogent. Marx and Engels frequently gloat over the changefulness of things. They deny that there are "eternal truths" and obviously think it naïve to hold that there is an unchangeable moral standard universally applicable to all men and all epochs. But they do not state their own view carefully or examine it with any rigour. They proclaim it rather as a means of discouraging and disheartening their opponents. Change and destruction fascinate them, stability they regard as uninteresting and contemptible if not impossible, and loyalty to the past as utterly misguided. *Mors immortalis*, "immortal death", is their gleefully uttered watchword.

But in spite of all this, the conception of some moral ideal haunts their writings. We have seen that *Capital* was intended to be a scientific analysis of the logic of capitalism, showing how it must work and how it must produce crises of increasing magnitude until it destroys itself. To say that capitalism is brutal is "sentimentality", to accuse the capitalist of injustice is beside the point. But we have also seen that Marx described capital as a werewolf and that a central conception of *Capital* is that in the capitalist system money dominates all, so that instead of men seeking to satisfy their reasonable needs they are enmeshed in an organization that has insatiable avarice as its driving force. R. H. Tawney in *Religion and the Rise of Capitalism* (1926) described Marx as "the last of the Schoolmen", and the account I have given of the argument of *Capital* supports this judgment—except that many writers since Marx, including Tawney himself, also criticize capitalism on the ground that it depends on greed. Thus Marx wishes to be "scientific" and only to describe, analyse and predict, yet on the other hand his descriptions turn into indictments, his analyses into condemnations and his predictions into prophecies. If he could have got his own way completely, there would have been no references to "truth, morality and justice" in the preamble to the rules of the First International. He is moralist and anti-moralist in one, perhaps an anti-moralistic moralist. Can we, then, find out more about his attitude towards morality and about the nature of his moral convictions?

One place in which we may look is the *Economic and Philosophical Manuscripts of 1844,* which we mentioned in Chapter 3, §2 above. Since these manuscripts were first published, they have been widely quoted, although less widely expounded and discussed, and a word frequently used in them, "alienation", has by now become something of a catchword. The word itself was familiar to Marx from the writings of Hegel and of Feuerbach, both of whom had been struck by the fact that men's own creations take on a form that appears independent of their creator. We have seen that this is how Feuerbach regarded God and the spirit world; they were human creations which their creators, however, regarded as independent of them, and in consequence the human being is divided into two, into a real being here on earth and an imaginary being beyond the world. Feuerbach believed that men could only free themselves from this alienation and become effective unitary beings by disillusioning themselves of their false beliefs. Marx believed that this disillusionment could only take place when the world had been so altered that religious beliefs were no longer needed. In the 1844 *Manuscripts*, however, after he had come under the influence of Engels, he applied this idea in the economic sphere. Men's lives consist of the things they do, the labour they perform, the things they bring about by means of this labour, but in capitalist society money plays the part of a sort of god which sees to it that men's labour does them no good but is sacrificed to a cruel impersonal Mammon. When the worker has to produce commodities for sale, the fruits of his labour are, in the legal sense, "alienated" from him, *i.e.* made the property of another. Furthermore, he has to sell his labour itself, and hence the very essence of his life does not belong to him. He labours for an impersonal market, he does not get what he makes, and he lives his working life in the service of someone else. In primitive society men lived in caves because they couldn't find anything better, but in modern capitalist society they live in cave-like dwellings because the money economy prevents them from living anywhere else. Marx also used the word "estrangement" to describe the situation of individual men in capitalist society. Society is not something that corresponds to their needs and desires, but is a hostile, menacing, impersonal system in which they feel lost.

Estrangement appears in that *my* means of life belong to someone else, in that what *I* wish for is the inaccessible possession of *someone else*. It appears also in that everything is always something *other* than itself, in that my activity is *something else*, and, finally, in that in general *inhuman* power is supreme.

If we disregard the somewhat self-pitying tone (like A. E. Housman, Marx is indignant that he has been born "in a world I never made"), we can extract certain basic presuppositions of Marx's view. The complaint that individuals have to sell their labour and hence themselves, presupposes the ideal of men who are their own masters and who can express themselves in their work without having to conform to an impersonally organized system. What Marx seems to have wished for was a society in which individuality was given the fullest scope. He also wished for a society in which there was no concealment. In capitalist society, he believed, people did not really know what they were doing, since each man's individual effort contributed to a total outcome and was part of a system of relationships of which he had little or no understanding. Marx believed that freedom of contract was a disguise that concealed capitalist domination, and he wished to strip off the disguise and restore the independence of individuals. But this, he held, could only be done by so arranging things that the social system comes under the conscious control of co-operating individuals. His principal aims seem to have been independence, creativity, self-awareness and co-operation. He thought it bad that individuals should be divided in their own personalities and at odds with one another. The unalienated individual would know what he was doing, would do it in concert with his fellows, and would live in a social world that men had organized for themselves and could feel at home in.

An equally important document for an understanding of Marx's moral outlook is *The Holy Family*. This book is particularly important because it throws light on what I have called Marx's ambivalence towards morality, that is, his frequently asserted desire to have nothing to do with it, and his prophetic indignation at the injustices and cruelties of his time. In *The Holy Family* Marx quotes from a book by the French socialist, Fourier, entitled *Théorie des Quatre Mouvements* (1808). Fourier held that men's natural instincts (or passions, as he called them, in the terminology of his day) should not be repressed, as moralists of all ages had recommended, but should be given the freest possible expression. Fourier used the word "moralism" for this false view (as he held it to be) that the passions should be repressed, and wrote: "what is it (morality) in the body of the sciences, if not the fifth wheel of the coach, powerlessness in action? Whenever morality fights on its own against a vice, one can be sure that it will be defeated". Marx quotes this passage in one of the chapters of *The Holy Family*, written by him and not by Engels. Like Fourier, Marx believed that the social order should be made suitable to the nature of man, not the nature of man suppressed in order to conform to the social order. Like Fourier, he believed that appeals to right and duty effected nothing and that, instead of denouncing and blaming, men should find out what makes men unhappy and introduce the means of satisfying their desires. Marx said in *The Holy Family* that materialism is "the logical basis of communism". By this he meant that men are shaped by their circumstances and environment, so that if they are to fulfil their natures they must alter their environment, they must "form their circumstances so as to make them human". Marx makes it clear, elsewhere in the book, that he disapproved of retribution, of expiation and of remorse. He disapproved of these things because he believed that they repressed and depressed the natural instincts and desires. Instead of blaming and punishing wrongdoers, the social circumstances which led to crime should be transformed. Indeed, Marx rather approved of those criminals who rebelled against the capitalist system of property and respectability. To punish such people was to suppress human vitality, and to make them sorry for what they had done was to turn them into subservient hypocrites.

This sort of view is much more prevalent in our day than it was when Marx put it forward. Psychiatrists have enlarged on the dangers to the personality of too great repression of the instinctive urges, and penal reformers have argued that punishment should be mitigated or even abolished altogether. "Fulfilment" is regarded by many as an adequate and even as an admirable ideal. But like Marx, "reformers" of this type do not fail to be indignant when people advocate repression of the instinctive desires or justify severe punishment on retributive grounds. They cannot help believing that the advocates of repression must be suppressed or circumvented. There are some sorts of fulfilment that they are most anxious to prevent. Marx, in the passage from *The Holy Family* about French materialism and morality, says that the materialist (whom he approves) is in favour of "well-understood interest" and of "the positive power to assert his true individuality". At the end of the chapter in which he says this he includes as a sort of appendix some quotations from Helvétius, d'Holbach and Bentham. A paragraph from d'Holbach and a passage from Bentham are of particular interest to us here. That from d'Holbach reads: "Man can never separate himself from himself for a single instant in his life: he cannot lose sight of himself." That from Bentham reads: "Individual interests are the only real interests." It is clear that Marx's ideal was that of unrepressed, completely fulfilled individual men. It was an ideal which commended itself to many of the "philosophers" of eighteenth-century France. The difficulty in it, of course, is that some men, if unrepressed, would injure other men, and their fulfilment would be at the expense of other men's fulfilment. Professor L. G. Crocker, in his *An Age of Crisis* (1959), points out that this emphasis on self-interest reached its supreme expression in the words and works of the Marquis de Sade who wrote: "Give me a being in the world who by his nature can be exempt of all humanity's ills; not only will that being not feel any kind of pity, he will not be able even to conceive it." Why should not the man who enjoys cruelty perpetrate it? Because, of course, it causes others to suffer unwanted pain. Then the sadist must be held in check and this means rules, laws, morality, punishment, sadists who have to repress their sadism. No doubt Marx believed that no one is naturally a sadist, that it is society alone that makes men cruel. But we do not know that this is so and therefore we do not know what would happen in a society of unrepressed men. Fulfilment is a dangerous as well as a vague ideal. If, as Marx held, the fulfilment must be that of men united together for their common good, then much that individuals would want to do has to be repressed, and we are back with duty and renunciation once more.

6 Conclusion

I have endeavoured to give a brief critical exposition of
the views of the man whose name has been given to a
movement which has had an historical impact greater
perhaps than that of Calvinism and comparable with that
of Protestantism as a whole. If this exposition is correct,
then we must conclude that there are serious vaguenesses
and inconsistencies in Marx's teachings. The precise
import, for example, of the central theory, that of historical
materialism, cannot be determined, although the historical
importance of technology and economic organization is
beyond question, and Marx was right to emphasize it.
Again, Marx's economic theory is expressed in an obsolete
idiom, and is permeated by a moral disapproval which he
was anxious to deny. Some of Marx's social predictions,
those, for example, about increasing technological con-
centration, have come off, while others, notably the
prediction that the rich would get richer and the poor

poorer, seem a long way from being fulfilled. The social system that Marx attacked between 1844 and 1883 no longer exists. Keynes revived and revised ideas such as those of Sismondi and Malthus so as to get rid of the under-consumption that gave rise to dangerous economic crises, and in consequence capitalism, although now in a neo-mercantilist form, continues in existence. That is to say, the pursuit of profit continues as an essential feature of the economic system, even though there is much interference, some of it ill-considered, with the workings of the market.

But although the problem of under-consumption seems to have been overcome, other problems have taken its place and may prove just as difficult to solve. The continuance of predominantly capitalist institutions has not prevented great advances in the quantity and (in some cases) quality of output, and although followers of Marx say that greater advances would have been made under communism, this has not been shown, and perhaps could not be. Furthermore, a strange paradox has been enacted. In Britain, France, Germany and the United States, countries where capitalism has been highly developed, the system has not collapsed, and communist society has not been inaugurated. But in Russia and in China, countries where there was comparatively little capitalist development, forms of socialist societies have been set up under the control of men who accept the doctrines of Marx. Thus, men whose conviction it is that new ideas and ideals are the results of industrial and economic changes have utilized Marx's ideas and ideals to institute great industrial and economic changes. Events in the communist countries of the world, therefore, do not seem to give support to the Marxist doctrines which their governments profess. On the contrary, Marx's doctrines seem to be disproved by the events they have given rise to. How has this strange thing come about? It would take many volumes to try to answer this question. But we may make some guesses about the answer to another question: What is it in Marx's writings that can have favoured such an outcome?

I suggest that the central and decisive feature of Marx's theory that tended in this direction was the historical importance he attributed to the proletariat. We have seen that in his 1844 essay on Hegel's *Philosophy of Right* Marx said that the proletariat was the revolutionary class, that it would be the heart of the future revolution and that philosophy (*i.e.* Marx's ideas) would be its head. Marx then said that the revolution would be made by and on behalf of those who had an interest in overthrowing the existing social order. He and Engels thereupon constituted themselves the proletariat's intellectual Egeria. They provided the proletariat's natural passions with reasons, or at least with rationalizations. Marx was not alone, in the first half of the nineteenth century, in realizing the power that the working classes possessed. In various writings Carlyle had emphasized this. In his *French Revolution* (1837), for example, he had repeatedly referred to the way in which "the people" rose against the burdens that had been placed on them, and in *Past and Present* there are references to an undercurrent of popular menace. Earlier than this, Saint-Simon had observed that if unemployment was allowed to develop to too great proportions, the workers might be tempted to attack the existing order. Marx maintained that capitalism could not exist without unemployment. Exploitation, he held, was essential to it, and improvement or reform of it quite impossible. He thus provided a rationale for proletarian activity. If Mr. Cremer and other workers' leaders did not have this conception of their role in history, they were nevertheless to be guided by men who did.

From their correspondence we may learn how Marx and Engels kept in touch with working-class organizations all over Europe and did their best to control them and to denigrate anyone who opposed their views. While Engels was still alive, Lenin read Volume I of *Capital*, the *Anti-Dühring* and *The Holy Family*, a book which at that time was very little known. It is interesting to notice that in Chapter VI of *The Holy Family* there is a discussion of the role which the masses are to play in the future of mankind, and it was Lenin's view that it is the masses who are to count for most as capitalism comes to its end. It was Lenin who put into practice this idea that the revolutionary leader must ascertain the needs and interest of the masses and make them irresistible. The masses, that is, all the dependent workers, whether on the land or in the factories, is a wider conception than that of the proletariat, but it was this wider conception that Lenin made use of when he gained power in Russia by siding with the Russian soldiers in demanding the peace for which they longed.

But if the masses were to be organized, this had to be done by the right people, that is, by those who shared Marx's understanding of capitalist society and his certainty that it would collapse. Marx was therefore very much concerned to refute rival socialist theories and to destroy the influence of leaders whose socialism differed from his own. The *Poverty of Philosophy* (1847) was hatchet-work of this sort, designed to humiliate Proudhon, who at that time was much better known than Marx—indeed, in *The Holy Family*, published two years earlier, Marx had expressed his admiration for Proudhon's famous book, *Qu'est-ce que la Propriété?* (1840). It is significant, too, that about a third of *The Communist Manifesto* itself consists of attacks on forms of socialism, including again that of Proudhon, with which Marx and Engels disagreed. We have seen, too, that the *Critique of the Gotha Programme* was in large part an attack on what Marx held were false conceptions of socialism. It is tempting to conclude from all this that Marx just was an assertive and quarrelsome man who could not brook opposition. But this is not so. What he was trying to do was to organize a movement that would conquer power for the proletariat, and he was determined not to be handicapped by half-hearted or other-minded associates. In a letter dated 9th April, 1870, Marx says that his daughter Jenny had got herself accepted as correspondent on Irish affairs for the French paper *La Marseillaise*. She did this by writing to the editorial board under the assumed name of Jenny Williams, and the incident might seem to be nothing but an amusing subterfuge. But the letter in which Marx writes of this is concerned with the attitude to be taken to Irish affairs by the First International. Marx says that England is at the time the most important capitalist country and therefore the country in which it is most important "to hasten the social revolution". The independence of Ireland would be a means of hastening this, and therefore the English workers should be made aware that Irish independence is not a "question of abstract justice or humanitarian feeling", but a step towards "their own social emancipation". Social revolution by the working class under the correct leadership was the aim to which everything else was subordinated. Before 1917 anyone reading Marx's and Engels' correspondence would have smiled at the quarrels and conspiracies they promoted and described. But when we read it now we see these same events as leading towards that union of proletarian heart and philosophical head which Marx had conceived in 1844.

It was because Proudhon disagreed with Marx's conspiratorial dogmatism that Marx broke with him. Marx had admired Proudhon's writings and seems to have met him and discussed with him in Paris in 1844–5. On 5th May, 1846, a letter signed by Marx, with two postscripts, one by Philippe Gigot and the other by Friedrich Engels, was sent to Proudhon from Brussels, asking him if he would collaborate with them in a correspondence that would keep French, German and English socialists in touch with one another and keep an eye on socialist writings and propaganda. In the postscript by Gigot it was stated that a certain Karl Grün, a German at that time living in Paris, was a charlatan and a parasite. Replying to this in a letter addressed to Marx himself, on the 17th May, Proudhon wrote:

Let us seek together, if you wish, the laws of society, the ways in which they are realized, the progress we make in discovering them; but, for God's sake, after having demolished all *a priori* dogmatisms, do not let us dream in our turn, of indoctrinating the people; do not let us fall into the contradiction of your compatriot Luther who, after having overturned the catholic theology, straightway started, with strong reinforcements of excommunications and anathemas, to establish a protestant theology.

As to Grün, Proudhon said that he had learnt from him about the writings of Marx and of Feuerbach and was anxious to employ him to translate one of his forthcoming books into German. Furthermore, he thought that Grün's attitude towards working men who consulted him was a guarantee of the rectitude of his intentions. The letter makes it quite clear that Proudhon fully understood Marx's aim of building up a cohesive, dogmatic group to "indoctrinate" the proletariat and lead it into violent revolution. In October 1846 Proudhon's *Philosophy of Poverty* appeared and provided Marx with the opportunity of attacking someone who might influence the workers in ways that Marx did not approve of.

Marx's writings, then, contained the doctrine which was to be used in preparing for proletarian revolution. Not only did Marx, along with Engels, state the doctrine, but he also, again with Engels, formed and fostered the group of men from which twentieth-century communism has developed.

Has Marx's *doctrine*, then, any importance apart from its connection with the Marxist socialist movement? It has certainly had considerable influence upon the growth of social theory, both by way of positive theories and by way of the reactions it gave rise to. After the publication of *Capital*, Volume I, Marx's economic theories attracted some attention and were criticized by such leading economists as Menger and Böhm-Bawerk. But the development of economic theory has taken a turn which renders Marx's theory of value and of surplus-value irrelevant, and even so sympathetic a critic as Professor Joan Robinson writes that "logically it is a mere rigmarole of words . . ." (*Economic Philosophy*, Penguin edition, 1964, p. 39).

What has influenced the development of social theory is the doctrine of historical materialism and, in particular, the theory of classes. The term "sociology" was invented by Auguste Comte, and sociology itself came into existence quite independently of Marx. But Max Weber (1864–1920), one of the greatest sociologists, was in part stimulated to enquiry by Marx's theory of history and of classes. Weber tried to show, for example, that capitalism came to pervade the social system only when and where certain religious and moral beliefs and attitudes favourable to it were already in being. This, of course, is to question, on historical grounds, Marx's view that the ideologies are produced by technological and economic factors. Discussion of this theme has led to further fruitful historical enquiries if not to greater historical understanding. Again, Weber believed that the state apparatus, and in particular the bureaucracy, is not merely an organization controlled by a ruling class as a means of maintaining itself in power, but is, in some circumstances, a power of its own, independent in some degree, of the class relationships that Marx had emphasized. Discussion of this theme has been a fruitful one for the development of sociology. Again, Marx thought that classes are objectively distinguishable entities corresponding to the division between landlords, capitalists and wage-earners. Whether classes can be distinguished in this objective way, or whether they depend rather upon people's *beliefs* about themselves and about their society, is another question that Marx's theory has given rise to by way of reaction. There is less readiness nowadays to take people's beliefs and statements at their face value than there was in Marx's day, and no doubt his theory of ideologies has worked in this direction. But, here, I suggest, the pioneer, for good and ill, was Feuerbach, who influenced not only Marx, but, in a later generation, Sigmund Freud.

Mention of Feuerbach brings us to Marx's attitude towards religion. Marx followed Feuerbach in holding that religious beliefs and hopes were a sort of imaginary wish-fulfilment. We have seen (Chapter 2, §2) that Marx described religion as a "halo" around the vale of sorrows we live in. Although Marx believed that religion is an outcome of poverty and hence of social conditions, his conception of it is expressed in psychological rather than social terms. He never seems to have considered religion as a social phenomenon with social functions. He looked upon it rather as a sort of hallucination which would fade away when society was reconstructed. If Marx had been more of a social investigator and less of a revolutionary, he might have asked how religious *institutions* are related to the other institutions of society, how they are related, for example, to growing up and to marriage, and how they are concerned with birth and with death. Machiavelli believed that the ancient Roman religion helped the Roman people to prosper and that Christianity was socially enervating. Possibly he was as much of an atheist as Marx was, but unlike Marx he perceived, with a cynical eye it is true, that religion is much more than a matter of sighs and wishes. Burke regarded it as a merit of the Christian religion that in it ruler and subjects were equally humbled before God, and that rulers were less likely, if they regard themselves as God's servants, to act tyrannically towards their people. But Marx's ideal did not comprise humility. Like Feuerbach, he regarded man as creator of the gods, and he considered the augmentation of human power to be the supreme end. In his doctoral dissertation, Marx had written: "Prometheus is the most distinguished saint and martyr in the philosophical calendar." He was a very young man when he wrote this, but this admiration for defying the gods on behalf of mankind remained with Marx all his life.

Thus there is no room in Marx's outlook for reverence towards superhuman powers. Marx had no feeling, either, for that *mysterium tremendum*, the sense of awe and admiration, which enters into some people's religious consciousness. His reaction to mystery was not awe but exasperation. In *The Holy Family* Marx has a lot to say about mysteries, partly because in that book he discusses Eugene Sue's novel, *The Mysteries of Paris*. Marx shows anger and contempt at those who make mysteries of things, who encourage "mystification". His aim, rather, is to reduce and eliminate mystery, so that men may be clear about the world and one another. In *Capital*, Volume I, there is a section (Ch. 1, §4) entitled "The Mystery of the Fetichistic Character of Commodities". Here Marx says that under the capitalist system the reality of social life is somehow concealed from men, and he looks forward to a time when "the relations between human beings in their practical everyday life have assumed the aspect of perfectly transparent and reasonable relations between man and man and between man and nature". Before this can be done, "the veil of mystery" will have to be torn off. We have the picture of a society of brisk and lucid men, confident that they know or can know everything that can concern them, amicably co-operating to keep nature and society under conscious control. There would seem to be no place in it for the dreamer, the mystic or the contemplative.

One strength of Marx's doctrine as regards its effectiveness as propaganda was that it was in accord with the direction in which things were going. In the eighteenth century a movement was started which had the extirpation of Christianity as its principal aim. The advocacy of individual fulfilment which reached its intellectual culmination in the writings of de Sade was only one side of an attempt to gain acceptance for the view that individual men are the supreme arbiters of their own satisfactions. This individualistic atheism was Marx's starting-point, the background to all he strove to attain. He never argued for it but started from it. Marx assumed that it was only the constraints and degradations of coercive social institutions that prevented men from developing all their powers in non-coercive association with one another. It was nature and institutions that had to be overcome, not man himself. It was society that had to be reorganized, not men who had to be restrained. This is not the same thing as the belief in the natural goodness of man. Marx did not think in such terms. The assumption, rather, is that men will spontaneously co-operate without coercion and without the need for resignation or self-sacrifice, once the last and worst form of social tyranny, the capitalist system, has been destroyed. The men who achieve this will be living in conditions of plenty, and since they will not have to compete with one another for a living, they will, Marx fancied, freely co-operate in fulfilling human potentialities.

We have seen that Marx was ready to engage in deception, and to justify bloodshed and the execution of hostages in order to hasten the advent of this alert, active, united community in which no one would experience religious awe or walk humbly or seek redemption. He had jibed at the Christian for making a division between the natural and the supernatural and between the body and the soul. But he himself was encouraging the formation of a more damaging division, that between the *existing* social system in which strife and hatred are in order, and a *future* society in which men quite different from ourselves will live lucid and uninhibited lives. But what is it to us what these men will do? Are not our tasks and our standards with us now?

Further Reading

Books of Selections

Karl Marx and Friedrich Engels: Selected Works. 2 vols. Moscow: Foreign Languages Publishing House; London: Lawrence and Wishart Ltd.

Marx and Engels: Basic Writings on Politics and Philosophy, ed. Lewis S. Feuer. New York: Doubleday, 1959.

Translations of Individual Works

Marx, Karl, and Engels, Friedrich. *The Communist Manifesto,* ed. Harold J. Laski. London: Allen & Unwin, 1948.

————. *The German Ideology.* Trans. by R. Pascal. London: Lawrence and Wishart Ltd.

Marx, Karl. *Capital.* Vol. I. Trans. by Eden and Cedar Paul, with an Introduction by G. D. H. Cole. New York: Dutton.

————. *Economic and Philosophical Manuscripts of 1844.* Trans. by Martin Milligan. Moscow: Foreign Languages Publishing House; London: Lawrence and Wishart Ltd. (This volume also contains a translation of Engels' *Sketch of a Critique of Political Economy*.)

There is another translation of the 1844 manuscripts, viz., *Karl Marx: Early Writings,* ed. and trans. by T. B. Bottomore. London: Watts, 1963; New York: McGraw-Hill, 1964. (This volume, like that edited by Feuer, above, contains a translation of Marx's *Critique of Hegel's Philosophy of Right*.)

There are translations of many other writings by Marx and Engels, some in the series published by the Foreign Languages Publishing House, Moscow.

The works of Marx and Engels are being published in German by Dietz Verlag, East Berlin.

Books about Marx and Marxism

Acton, H. B. *The Illusion of the Epoch: Marxism-Leninism as a Philosophical Creed*. London: Cohen and West, 1962.

Berlin, Sir Isaiah. *Karl Marx*. 3rd ed.: Oxford and New York: Oxford University Press, 1963.

Plamenatz, John. *German Marxism and Russian Communism*. London: Longmans; New York: Harper & Row, 1953.

———. *Man and Society*. Vol. II, chaps. 5 and 6. London: Longmans, 1961; New York: McGraw-Hill, 1963.

Popper, Sir Karl. *The Open Society and Its Enemies*. (*Hegel and Marx*, Vol. II.) 3rd ed.: Oxford: Oxford University Press, 1963.

Books about the History of Socialism

Cole, G. D. H. *The Forerunners, 1789-1850*. (*History of Socialist Thought*, 5 vols., Vol. I.) London: Macmillan; New York: St. Martin's Press, 1953.

———. *Marxism and Anarchism, 1850-90*. (*History of Socialist Thought*, Vol. II.) London: Macmillan; New York: St. Martin's Press, 1954.

Gray, Sir Alexander. *The Socialist Tradition*. London: Longmans, 1946.

Jackson, J. Hampden. *Marx, Proudhon and European Socialism*. London: English Universities Press; New York: Collier Books, 1957.

Index